Praise for *The Gardens of God*

"The strong pastoral and contemplative challenge of *The Gardens of God* invites reflection at many different levels, but its core message was summed up once in a brief, memorable statement by St. John Paul II: the minister of the Gospel 'must possess and pass on that "knowledge of God" which is not a mere deposit of doctrinal truths but a personal and living experience of the Mystery.'"

—**Paul Murray, OP**, Professor at the Pontifical University of St. Thomas Aquinas, from the foreword

"In the garden of humanity on the move, gardeners of the caliber of Cardinal Arthur Roche are striving to enliven the project of Jesus Christ to restore the world willed by the Creator, his Father. Tirelessly, Cardinal Roche sows in all hearts the words that give life; he heals wounds by pouring out the living water of the Holy Spirit; he recalls the Savior's promise to create a new earth, a lush garden forever saved by love, peace, and justice for all. This book is a true guide for any gardener who yearns to bear fruit in the garden of his own life."

—**Cardinal Gérald Lacroix**, Cardinal-Archbishop of Quebec, Canada

"Cardinal Roche offers us meditations on what are in effect archetypal biblical gardens. Remarkably, the entire arc of the story of salvation is enacted in these gardens, beginning in Eden and climaxing twice, first in the garden of the empty tomb of our Lord's Resurrection, and finally in the enclosed garden of each believer's heart. I am given hope as I move through these gardens, seeing in them what I might have otherwise missed without the cardinal as guide."

—**Abbot Jeremy Driscoll, OSB**, Abbot of Mount Angel Abbey

"In this thoughtful and well-crafted book, Cardinal Arthur Roche offers inspiring insights into the metaphorical image of the Church as God's garden. The nine chapters, beginning with 'Tending the Garden' and ending with 'The Enclosed Garden,' offer deep meditations that will nourish the faith journey of priests, religious, and laity alike."

—**Donna Orsuto**, Director of The Lay Centre at Foyer Unitas, Professor at the Pontifical Gregorian University

THE GARDENS OF GOD

THE GARDENS OF GOD

CARDINAL ARTHUR ROCHE

Foreword by Paul Murray, OP

WORD on FIRE.

Published by Word on Fire,
Elk Grove Village, IL 60007
© 2023 by Arthur Roche
Printed in the United States of America
All rights reserved

Cover design, typesetting, and interior art direction by
Nicolas Fredrickson and Marlene Burrell

26 25 24 23   1 2 3 4

ISBN: 978-1-68578-996-1

Library of Congress Control Number: 2022943338

Dedicated
to my Brother Priests

After the gift of this natural life, how can I yet again thank You, O Lord, for the even higher gift of faith and grace in which uniquely, at the end, my being finds its refuge? How can I worthily celebrate your goodness, O Lord, for having been immersed as soon as I entered this world into the ineffable Catholic Church? For being called and initiated into the Priesthood of Christ? For having had the joy and the mission of serving souls, brothers and sisters, the young, the poor, the people of God? And for having had the unmerited honour of being a minister of holy Church?

Testimony of Pope St Paul VI, 1965

Contents

Foreword

Fr Paul Murray, OP

This book has a very particular focus. It contains reflections preached by a cardinal archbishop to fellow priests
and bishops in different parts of the world. It is to them,
to the shepherds and leaders of God's people, that the
Word of God is here being proclaimed. The title of the
book is significant: *The Gardens of God*. Cardinal Roche
is concerned to remind us that priests and bishops are
called not only to be shepherds in God's kingdom; they
are called also to be gardeners in that kingdom, their
task to plant the seeds of living faith and cultivate the
plot of "land" given to them by providence – whether
that happens to be a parish or a diocese.

The image of the garden appears in an unusually
striking manner in both the Old and New Testaments.
In *The Gardens of God*, attention is given to five of these
appearances, each one more vivid than the previous: the
Garden of Eden, the Garden of Gethsemane, the Garden
of the Tomb, the Garden of Paradise, and the Enclosed
Garden. What becomes clear, as we read more of the

work, is that the different dimensions of faith experience, which these gardens represent, although they relate directly to the challenge of the priestly vocation, relate with no less directness and relevance to the vocation of each and every disciple of Christ. This means that the encouraging and radiant message of *The Gardens of God* can speak as much to the situation of the laity in the Church as to the lives of bishops and priests.

Those of us who may perhaps be undergoing great suffering, or who may suddenly be experiencing great joy, find named in the biblical images of Gethsemane and Eden something of our own experience as believers. And that is no small grace. But *The Gardens of God* encourages us, dares us, to think more radically about the meaning of these "gardens". We are encouraged to step back from our usual preoccupations and, in the light of these very powerful images, to reflect on who we are and to whom it is we belong. This task is one which, centuries ago, St Bernard of Clairvaux, writing in a long letter to the pope of that time, famously called "consideration". If, reading St Bernard's letter, we didn't know already to whom it was addressed, we might be inclined to think it was a message of earnest advice sent to a busy parish priest in our own time. One of its central teachings, a teaching repeated in *The Gardens of God*, is the critical importance of self-knowledge in the life of a busy pastor. The aim is not, of course, to replace the primary focus on God and neighbour with an exaggerated focus on the self. Far from it. Nevertheless, St Bernard of Clairvaux makes bold to say:

> If you wish to belong to others like him who became all things to all men, I will praise your humanity, but only if it is full. But how can it be full if you yourself are left out? You too are a man. So then, in order that your humanity may be full and complete, let your bosom, which receives all, find room also for yourself. . . . For if you are a stranger to yourself to whom are you not a stranger? . . . Remember, I do not say always, I do not say often, but at least sometimes render yourself to yourself.

Cardinal Roche refers more than once to the work of St Bernard, and to the work of many other saints and theologians. These "voices", far from distracting the reader, lend to the text an illumined quality and a wonderful depth and colour. And this, I would say, is particularly the case in the final chapter, "The Enclosed Garden", which celebrates the mystery of the Virgin Mary, viewing her, among other things, as exemplar and model of the life of contemplation.

Although no explicit references are made in *The Gardens of God* to the author's personal experience as priest and diocesan bishop, the authority and weight of that past experience are evident throughout – the knowledge of the bewilderment and desperation in the hearts of many of our contemporaries; the depth of their thirst for God; and the awareness of a shepherd's own need for continual, personal conversion and for an authentic life of prayer. The strong pastoral and contemplative challenge of *The Gardens of God* invites reflection at many different levels, but its core message was summed up once in a brief, memorable statement by St John Paul II: the minister of the Gospel "must possess and pass on that 'knowledge of God' which is not a mere deposit of doctrinal truths but a personal and living experience of the Mystery."

Preface

For pastors who live in circumstances which are personally challenging and where the general current of life, culturally as well as in other ways, hits hard against the teachings of Christ, there is an encouraging passage in the Acts of the Apostles. There we find St Paul facing the self-same difficulties that many bishops and priests face today. The city of Corinth was wealthy, the capital of the southern province of Greece under the rule of the Roman Empire. Its culture was sybaritic, its vices notorious, all of which affected its entire population. The hedonistic culture not only blurred but also had the capacity to suffocate much that was at the heart of the Gospel message. It was a deep disappointment to Paul and made him hesitate in his mission. However, in a dream it was revealed to him that despite the challenges there were good people there who were faithful and who needed to be cared for: "The Lord said to Paul one night in a vision, 'Do not be afraid, but go on speaking and do not be silent, for I am with you, and no one will attack you to harm you, for I have many in this city who are my people'" (Acts 18:9–10). It was enough for Paul to know this. He stayed and worked there and developed a special love for the Church he founded, despite later witnessing the decay which settled all too comfortably into its life like a poison ivy whose roots were buried deep on the outside yet whose tendrils were craftily invasive in penetrating the entire fabric.

When Paul later wrote his famous letters to them, he used the metaphor of 'God's field' to describe the Church (1 Cor 3:9), which resonates with Pope Francis' image of the Church today as a 'field hospital.' Amidst the wrangling over allegiances within the community, he reminded his hearers that while they had benefitted from the apostolic zeal of Paul who had planted the seeds of faith and Apollos who had watered those seeds, it was in fact God who had given the growth. Paul describes himself and Apollos as being at the service of the one who alone makes things grow. The entire Church is seen as a single field. Their respective roles, though different, had been given to them by God for the overall good. Both were needed, but it was God who was the true gardener.

What happened to the Christian community of Corinth sends a clear message to the Church in every age.

The chapters in this book, born in the main of conferences offered to bishops, priests, and seminarians in various parts of the world and at different times, offer some reflections based upon the metaphorical image of the Church as God's garden or field in which we encounter the pastoral challenges before us today. Greece was the world's first democracy whose way of thinking was imprinted upon its citizenship. Reflecting upon this, however, Paul counsels us against being formed by the patterns of this world, of drifting into sectarian polemics or divisive ideologies, and to see our task from a very different perspective.

✠AR

Tending the Garden

The secret of getting ahead is getting started.
Mark Twain

A story is told about a Desert Father who one day visited his neighbour to ask: "What is spiritual fatherhood?" The other thought for a while and then said: "One beggar telling another beggar where to get bread!"

The crumbs that are found in these pages have fallen from some of the bread which has been given to me to eat and which I have chewed upon at different moments and which has nourished me. In sharing them with you I act simply as a weather-beaten signpost whose only wish is to point to where the bread shop is!

These thoughts were prepared at different times for different audiences, but as I have been asked now to offer them to a wider readership, I do so aware that if these thoughts contain for others anything of genuine worth, then that is due to the inspiration of the Holy Spirit at work. Setting aside time each day for prayer and recollection allows us the opportunity to face God and to face ourselves in the light of God's presence. As we do this, it seems to me to be important that we should really try to face God rather than succumb to self-reflection. In reality, it is more important to think "Whose am I?" than "Who am I?" Before there can be a nominative, there has to be a genitive. Through creation, but particularly through Baptism, we belong to the Lord.

The answer to the question "Whose are we?" in fact, is not simply found within our own self-consciousness. We are not solely our own mystery; we are much bigger than that! We belong to God who is beyond our measure and in whose image we are made. But part of the answer also lies with those to whom we have been sent to serve as ministers of his Good News.

It is clear that a bishop's identity is most evident when he stands at the altar with his priests and people gathered around him. There his priesthood is clearly seen as he intercedes for the Church and the entire world as he re-enacts the sacrifice of Calvary. In the Roman Canon, we learn that the bishop is one who, "holding to the truth, hands on the catholic and apostolic faith." This English translation, however, doesn't capture the entire meaning of the Latin text. *Orthodoxis atque catholicae et apostolicae* is a description of bishops, who are defined as *fidei cultoribus*, the ones who cultivate and hand on the Catholic and Apostolic faith.

The word *cultor* comes from the Latin verb *colo, colere*, which means 'to cultivate'. A *cultor fidei* is someone who cultivates faith like a gardener cultivates the land. He is someone who plants a tree in the soil that reaches to the heavens! The word 'column', interestingly, has the same derivation. Classical architecture makes it easy for us to recognise trees in the magnificent columns of Greece and Rome where we see before our eyes stone trunks of trees whose capitals bear the semblance of branches and foliage.

The *cultor* is someone who plants and harvests, who works and cares for the crops, the vines, who keeps bees and tends the beasts. These are all the original Latin usages. So, from within the context of the Eucharistic Prayer, we can say that bishops and priests are gardeners and farmers, as well as shepherds! They have to work at ground level, in the dust, among the weeds in God's field.

The *cultor* belongs to the land, which is one of the reasons why bishops have a specific territory in their titles. It is there, in his territory, that he plants and cultivates and brings in the harvest. He is someone who supports and fosters, who teaches and guides and guards against fraudulency.

In Latin there is another verb, *colo, colāre* – in contrast to *colo, colere* – which is not of the same root. This verb speaks, however, of someone who adores and reverences God, who is devoted to God and zealous in his faith. In this ancient Roman sense, he is a priest of the deity he serves. And as a priest he is the one who gives right faith to God, which is the meaning of *orthodoxus*.

What, after all, is Apollos? And what is Paul? Only servants, through whom you came to believe – as the Lord has assigned to each his task. I planted the seed, Apollos watered it, but God has been making it grow. So neither the one who plants nor the one who waters is anything, but only God, who makes things grow. The one who plants and the one who waters have one purpose, and they will each be rewarded according to their own labour. For we are co-workers in God's service; you are God's field, God's building. (1 Cor 3:5–9)

The image of the gardener or the cultivator is one that in the Scriptures is originally reserved to God – "for there was no man to work the ground", as we hear in the book of Genesis (Gen 2:5). The very first example of God's cultivation of the land is when he breathes on the soil, blowing his spirit into the dust of the earth and forming the first man, Adam, who, with Eve, was the summit of his creation. Following on from this, God establishes and cultivates a garden – "the LORD God planted a garden in Eden, in the east" (Gen 2:8). St Basil the Great tells us that this is the reason why there was a tradition of praying towards the east, expressing a longing to return to our homeland, to paradise.

Out of the ground the LORD God made to grow every tree that is pleasant to the sight and is good for food, the tree of life also in the midst of the garden, and the tree of the knowledge of good and evil. (Gen 2:9)

After establishing this fertile patch, God then places man into this garden, handing over to him the responsibility to cultivate it further – "to till it and keep it" (Gen 2:15).

St Ephrem the Syrian and St Augustine of Hippo explain that Eden, of course, is the land of paradise that God made after he created man. It is also a symbol of the Church that needs tending and into which he places the human race.

Against the immense and unfolding drama of creation in chapter 1 of Genesis – so beautifully depicted in the Sistine Chapel – and against the broad brushstrokes of bringing into being light and darkness, the swirling waters and the appearance of land, we suddenly find ourselves, in the second and third chapters, in a beautiful garden of tranquillity, which even God enjoys as he walks through it in the evening, savouring its delights. Of course, it did not last very long! The sin of our first parents brought this idyllic moment to an end. Nevertheless, what is interesting here, St Ephrem in his commentary tells us, is that the reason why God's footsteps could be heard was in order to help our first parents – as it were, to give them a chance to make supplication to God. Instead, they hid. St John Chrysostom, however, says that the sound of God walking was to induce a fear in them for what they had done. These two opinions perhaps highlight well the difference between a deacon and a bishop! Ephrem says that had they sought to repent at this moment, even though not regaining what they had lost through their sinfulness, God's heart would have softened and they would have escaped the curses decreed upon them and the earth.

Gardens are important. The places where we plant and gather the harvest speak to us of life and livelihood. There are quite a number of gardens specifically mentioned in the Bible. Among them, the Garden of Eden, of course, which later the prophet Ezekiel calls 'God's garden' (Ezek 28:13, 31:8–9) and Isaiah the 'Garden of the Lord' (Isa 51:3); the vineyard of Naboth that Ahab wanted to change into a vegetable garden for his own use (1 Kgs 21); the enclosed garden where Susanna bathed and was maliciously accused by lecherous old men (Dan 13); the locked garden in the Song of Songs which is likened to the Bride (Sg 4:12); and the many allegorical sketches that we find in the prophets, not least in Isaiah and Jeremiah.

But there are in particular four gardens which play an important part in God's own drama from Genesis to the Apocalypse. First, the Garden of Eden – 'God's garden' – which became the garden of sin. Second, the Garden of Gethsemane (Mt 26:36, Mk 14:32), literally meaning 'oil press' and well known as a place of prayer, which became the garden of suffering. Then, third, the Garden of the Tomb (Jn 19:41), which became the garden of victory. We should not overlook the fact that it was a new tomb, a virgin tomb, which symbolises for the Fathers of the Church a womb from which a new birth took place. The cultivation of this garden, through Baptism, is made very clear in the Third Eucharistic Prayer where, praying for the dead, we say, "Who was united [*complantatus fuit*] with your Son in a death like his, may also be one with him in his Resurrection." But the phrase *complantatus fuit* (keeping Romans 6:5 in mind), actually means that in Baptism, which is derived from the verb "to plunge", we are planted in the same furrow of the earth, as it were, in which Christ was planted in death in order to rise with him to life. And finally, there is the Garden of Paradise, the garden of eternal life, the garden where the new tree of life, the cross, bears the fruit which is Christ's Body. This garden is where the complete gathering of the Church takes place even now as well as at the end of time.

The specific character of these gardens is to be found in each diocese and in each community. Indeed, they are to be found in the gardens of every soul.

I shall use these images in order to reflect upon the question of 'whose we are'. It may be that you feel closer to one than to another, but all of them will play a part in our life and in the lives of our priests and people, and each one of them will speak about 'whose we are'. St Paul reminds us of our responsibility regarding this when to the church of Corinth he wrote:

> Do not forget: thin sowing means thin reaping; the more you sow, the more you reap. Each one should

give what he has decided in his own mind, not grudgingly or because he is made to, for God loves a cheerful giver. And there is no limit to the blessings which God can send you – he will make sure that you will always have all you need for yourselves in every possible circumstance, and still have something to spare for all sorts of good works. As scripture says: He was free in almsgiving, and gave to the poor: his good deeds will never be forgotten. The one who provides seed for the sower and bread for food will provide you with all the seed you want and make the harvest of your good deeds a larger one, and, made richer in every way, you will be able to do all the generous things which, through us, are the cause of thanksgiving to God. For doing this holy service is not only supplying all the needs of the saints, but it is also increasing the amount of thanksgiving that God receives. By offering this service, you show them what you are, and that makes them give glory to God for the way you accept and profess the gospel of Christ, and for your sympathetic generosity to them and to all. And their prayers for you, too, show how they are drawn to you on account of all the grace that God has given you. Thanks be to God for his inexpressible gift! (2 Cor 9:6–15)

Perhaps the thought of entering one or other of these gardens may cause us to hesitate, maybe through fear of what we may find or have to face there, tempting us to move on to a greener pasture or to a more colourful place. This, of course, is the residual mark of original sin – the contagion which has left us with an instinct within to hide. Like Adam and Eve who "heard the sound of the Lord God walking in the garden in the cool of the day . . . [and] hid themselves from the presence of the Lord God among the trees of the garden" (Gen 3:8), we too need to be attentive to the sound of God's feet and be encouraged by that sound rather than hide because of it. Resisting the instinct to turn the other way, Eli's counsel to Samuel when God had called out to the young man in the night encourages us to be attentive. "'What was it that he told you?'" said Eli, referring to God. "'Do not hide it from me.' . . . So Samuel told him everything and hid nothing from him. And [Eli] said, 'It is the Lord!' . . . And Samuel grew, and the Lord was with him and he let none of his words fall to the ground" (1 Sm 3:17–19). We always grow stronger by facing reality. With the Psalmist, we can pray, deep within our hearts, "It is your face O LORD that I seek, hide not your face from me" (Ps 27:8–9). It is a good prayer for us to utter. God is to be found in all these places, as he has demonstrated, and where God is we need have no fear.

The Song of Songs tells us:

> My beloved has gone down to his garden
> to the beds of spices,
> to graze in the gardens
> and to gather lilies.

I am my beloved's and my beloved is mine.
(Sg 6:2–3)

We will find God in each one of these gardens, and they will give us an insight into whose we are and whose we are yet still to become.

Laying Down the Foundations

God gives every bird its food, but
He does not throw it into its nest.
Josiah Gilbert Holland

Every garden must have a place of storage. In our service as gardeners in the kingdom of God, I would like to suggest that we must build a house or a hut in which to dwell in the garden, but which must be built on firm foundations.

"When you pray, you must not be like the hypocrites; for they love to stand and pray in the synagogues and at the street corners, that they may be seen by men. Truly, I say to you, they have received their reward. But when you pray, go into your room and close the door and pray to your Father who is in secret; and your Father who sees in secret will reward you. And in praying do not heap up empty phrases as the Gentiles do; for they think that they will be heard for their many words. Do not be like them, for your Father knows what you need before you ask him. Pray then like this: Our Father who art in heaven, Hallowed be thy name. Thy kingdom come. Thy will be done, on earth as it is in heaven. Give us this day our daily bread; and forgive us our debts, as we also have forgiven our debtors; and lead us not into temptation, but deliver us from evil. For if you forgive men their trespasses, your heavenly Father also will forgive you; but if you do not forgive men their trespasses, neither will your Father forgive your trespasses." (Mt 6:5–15)

If you have ever felt at sea, adrift, dissatisfied, feeling that nothing really satisfies your deeper, inner longings; if you have felt lonely and incomplete; if you question what life is about and yet feel that there is more to it, then you know what it is to live as an exile – perhaps even a stranger in your own land. It is the experience of every pilgrim, indeed of every human being. Gabriel Marcel, the French existentialist philosopher, warned that when a man is completely satiated, he is like an apple that is perfectly ripe. There is only one more stage left – and that is to rot! For Marcel, self-satisfaction brings good things to a bad end. Chesterton recognised that completeness and comfort are almost the definitions of insanity! "There is but an inch of difference", he said, "between the cushioned chamber and the padded cell!"

The itinerant preacher whose sermon we find in the Letter to the Hebrews knew how important this sense of longing is to our lives as a guiding spirit that, in its search and deep ache for something greater, leads us to God – not a distant God but a God who liberates us from ourselves, our self-preoccupation, who saves us, whose warmth is really the only thing ever to satisfy our deepest desires.

What a powerfully engaging orator he must have been as he preached at the crossroads and on the highways of Israel to people who lived with their own inner poverty, yet yearned in their hearts for something greater and which made sense of all they experienced:

Now faith is the assurance of things hoped for, the conviction of things not seen. For by it the people of old received their commendation. By faith we understand that the universe was created by the word of God, so that what is seen was not made out of things that are visible. . . . By faith Noah, being warned by God concerning events as yet unseen, in reverent fear constructed an ark for the saving of his household. By this he condemned the world and became an heir of the righteousness that comes by faith. By faith Abraham obeyed when he was called to go out to a place that he was to receive as an inheritance. And he went out, not knowing where he was going. By faith he went to live in the land of promise, as in a foreign land, living in tents with Isaac and Jacob, heirs with him of the same promise. For he was looking forward to the city that has foundations, whose designer and builder is God. . . . These all died in faith, not having received the things promised, but having seen them and greeted them from afar, and having acknowledged that they were strangers and exiles on the earth. . . . By faith Moses, when he was born, was hidden for three months by his parents, because they saw that the child was beautiful, and they were not afraid of the king's edict. By faith Moses, when he was grown up, refused to be called the son of Pharaoh's daughter, choosing rather to be mistreated with the people of God than to enjoy the fleeting pleasures of sin. He considered abuse suffered for the Christ greater wealth than the treasures of Egypt, for he was looking to the reward. (Heb 11:1–3, 7–10, 13, 23–26)

Each of these patriarchal figures – our ancestors in the faith – experienced this deep longing. Indeed, through grace, they longed for something greater than could be foreseen, for they were longing for Christ, which is amazing! Their longing was suffused with faith. It gave them an inner eye to see Christ in the far distance and gave them the ability to do the things they did, extraordinary, heroic things, because of him – not least, the complete abandonment of themselves, the courage of setting out on journeys not knowing where they were going, their only tools of navigation being a deep inner trust in the Lord. They were in fact more than heroic, because it was not given to them to see what we see and experience as a result of the Incarnation. And still we do not yet see it all; we see so little.

Moses, for example, led others to the Promised Land, saw it, but did not enter it (Nb 20:12). He brought forth water from the rock, but it was not for himself. He was to receive something greater, something that was hidden from view. God gave him the Promised Land of heaven, not of earth, and the life-giving water that flows from the heart of Christ for whom he had suffered, although never seen.

The lives of bishops and priests can be like that, too. We do a lot of things in our ministry the effects of which we never see. One sows, another reaps. Moses pleaded for the stubborn people God had chosen; he suffered for them, led them despite all their bickering and rebelliousness, but in the end, it was Joshua who led them into the Promised Land, not Moses. He only saw the land from afar. He lived by faith.

We have all known bishops and priests who spend their time and energies doing everything in their power, and with deep faith, to evangelise and bring their communities alive – and it is sometimes an uphill battle and a thankless task with no visible result. Another follows on, and it all begins to blossom. It springs into life seemingly with little effort on his part. But the second phase cannot happen without the first, and both are moments for faith and of a special grace. Indeed, such things are incomprehensible without faith. One sows, another reaps. The call is not to celebrity status but to service, much of it hidden, never known about. Whose work is it, in reality? Who is it, after all, for whom we are working? What part do we play? Whose are we? We are simply co-workers, not master builders (see Is 27:3). One sows, another reaps, and the Lord's work is accomplished in this humble way. When a preacher of the Gospel points to himself, well, that is where it stops – at the level of self. It isn't for us to do that; our task, whether as a sower or a reaper, is to point to Christ, to be signposts to a greater reality than ourselves. It is one of the reasons why we are to live chastely as celibates – all the time all that is within us truly pointing to Christ, longing for him, even as we struggle with our natural yearnings. All of this is part of what the Fourth Eucharistic Prayer calls "bringing to perfection his work in the world," so that "he might sanctify creation to the full." We simply have a small part to play in it all, or, as Cardinal Newman so beautifully expressed in his meditation:

> God has created me to do Him some definite service; He has committed some work to me which He has not committed to another. I have my mission – I never may know it in this life, but I shall be told it in the next. Somehow I am necessary for His purposes, as necessary in my place as an Archangel in his – if, indeed, I fail, He can raise another, as He could make the stones children of Abraham. Yet I have a

part in this great work; I am a link in a chain, a bond of connexion between persons. He has not created me for naught. I shall do good, I shall do His work; I shall be an angel of peace, a preacher of truth in my own place, while not intending it, if I do but keep His commandments and serve Him in my calling. Therefore I will trust Him. Whatever, wherever I am, I can never be thrown away. If I am in sickness, my sickness may serve Him; in perplexity, my perplexity may serve Him; if I am in sorrow, my sorrow may serve Him. My sickness, or perplexity, or sorrow may be necessary causes of some great end, which is quite beyond us. He does nothing in vain; He may prolong my life, He may shorten it; He knows what He is about. He may take away my friends, He may throw me among strangers, He may make me feel desolate, make my spirits sink, hide the future from me – still He knows what He is about.

This is a theme to which Pope Francis often refers. At a gathering of newly ordained bishops in Rome, he told them:

Remember that God was already present in your dioceses when you arrived and will still be there when you are gone. And, in the end, we will all be measured not on the accounting of our works but on the growth of God's work in the heart of the flock that we keep in the name of the "Shepherd and keeper of our souls" (cf. 1 Pt 2:25).

The prayer of longing which comes from the heart connects us with the long procession throughout the ages of distinguished servants of God who longed for the Lord and who lived as we also do today within the poverty of our own lives – a poverty that longs for something greater.

In Matthew's Gospel, the command to "go into your room" contains the phrase *eiserchesthai eis*, "to enter, to go into". In the book of Exodus, Aaron entered into the Holy Place; later on, Acts and Hebrews speak of going into the temple (Ex 28:29, Ac 3:3 etc., Heb 9:6 etc.). The phrase 'enter into' is important, because this is what God invited the patriarchs and the prophets to do also, and it was by this that their faith, their trust, was strengthened by entering into and encountering God personally in prayer and not allowing themselves to hide from that encounter. This is where we find the secret of our lives. "When you pray", says our Lord, "go to your inner room [enter deep within yourself], close the door, and pray to your Father in secret. And your Father who sees in secret will repay you" (Mt 6:5–6). It reminds us of what God said to his faithful servant Moses in the book of Exodus: "There I will meet you" (Ex 25:22). We recognize it also in the Psalms: "God is within" (Ps 46:5). We are told that it was there that "the Lord spoke to Moses face to face as a man speaks to his friend" (Ex 33:11). It is interesting to note that in the book of Numbers we read that God speaks with Moses "mouth to mouth" (Nb 12:8). This encourages us to enter consciously into this place of *rendez-vous*. "I will not leave you desolate, I will come to you" (Jn 14:18), says Jesus. "Whoever comes to me I will not cast out" (Jn 6:37). This movement is the work of the Holy Spirit who led Simeon, as we hear it recorded in Luke's Gospel, "to the temple, inspired by the Spirit" (Lk 2:27), to meet Jesus. We too are the temples where we meet Jesus. As the prophet Malachi puts it, "The Lord whom you seek will suddenly come to his temple" (Ml 3:1).

The notion of "there I will meet you" is remarkably fulfilled through the Incarnation, which allows us, too, to say with Peter who was with Jesus on the mountain, "Lord, it is good for us to be here" (Lk 9:33).

The story of Gideon in the book of Judges reveals something of God's gentle patience in the face of our hesitations. When we concentrate on ourselves in his presence rather than on him, our smallness can give way to distrust. You will recall how Gideon was chosen to overcome the immense army that ranked against Israel with only a handful of men to help him. In the final moments of their conversation, the Lord says to him:

> "Go in the strength now upholding you, and you
> will rescue Israel from the power of Midian. Do
> I not send you myself?" Gideon answered him,
> "Forgive me, my Lord, but how can I deliver Israel?

My clan, you must know, is the weakest in Manasseh and I am the least important in my family." The LORD answered him, "I will be with you and you shall crush Midian as though it were a single man." Gideon said to him, "If I have found favour in your sight, give me a sign that it is you who speak to me. I beg you, do not go away until I come back. I will bring you my offering and set it down before you." And he answered, "I will stay until you return." (Jg 6:14–18)

We put off praying, preferring to do other things, but God waits patiently until we return!

People often said of Cardinal Basil Hume, who was Archbishop of Westminster from 1976–1999 and was a Benedictine monk, that he didn't live in a monastic cell but that he carried the monastic cell around within himself. He was a man of deep prayer, and his prayerfulness could be sensed. There was a stillness at his core which for others was like a window into God's world. St Ambrose, commenting on Matthew's Gospel, says that "the Apostle teaches us to pray everywhere, while the Saviour says 'Go into your room'. But you must not think that he means by this a room with four walls that separates you physically from others, but the room, the secret space within you in which your thoughts are enclosed and where your feelings are. That is your prayer-room, always with you wherever you are, always secret wherever you are, and what happens there is witnessed by God alone."

"When you pray, enter . . ." This is the first concrete and intimate invitation from the Lord – "enter" – more intimate than his first summons to "come and see" (Jn 1:39). This is something much more personal, for we have to go within ourselves. Jesus' parable of the tax collector and the Pharisee captures well the consequence of resisting this invitation and remaining on the outside: "'God, I thank you'", said the Pharisee, "'that I am not as the rest of men, extortioners, unjust, adulterers, or even as this publican. I fast twice in the week; I give tithes of all that I get.' But the publican, standing afar off, would not lift up so much as his eyes unto heaven, but smote his breast, saying, 'God, be merciful to me a sinner.' I say unto you, this man went down to his house justified" (Lk 18:11–14a).

We have all been on the outside at one time or another. When Judas betrayed the Lord, he "went outside; and it was night" (Jn 13:30). "Throw this useless servant into the darkness outside, where there will be wailing and grinding of teeth" (Mt 25:30), says Jesus in Matthew's Gospel, in contrast to "Enter into the joy of your Master" (Mt 25:21, 23). The older brother of the prodigal son refused to enter the feast (Lk 15:28). "Strive to enter through the narrow gate" says Jesus (Lk 13:24). The Greek verb *agonizesthe* (strive) is strong. The personal Passover of every person towards this interior feast of encounter comes through the "agony" of fighting and, not least, fighting against all the excuses to do anything else but 'enter into'.

The entire biblical drama is re-enacted in each person who strives and longs to enter the Promised Land of interior prayer. The parable of the Great Banquet ends with the words "Force them to enter" (Lk 14:23), which capture the Lord's personal longing for us to enter and his own earnestness for this encounter to take place. There is an agony and a struggle before the discovery. You will recall well how St Augustine wrote in his *Confessions*: *Et ecce intus eras et ego foris et ibi te quaerebam* – "And behold, you were within and I outside and it was there that I sought you [but you were not]."

We all know and experience this struggle and this longing. How often we pray, "O God, you are my God, for you I long. My soul thirsts for you like a dry weary land without water" (Ps 63:2). We understand what it is to feel desiccated and fallow.

Longing is, in reality, God's Spirit enticing us to 'enter in' and to meet him there. St Teresa of Calcutta said something to the effect that our very desire to pray is in fact prayer. It is already the presence of the Holy Spirit beckoning us to enter into his presence.

As we mull this over in our minds, a useful prayer, indeed a resolution, for us to utter throughout the day is "I will not . . . get into my bed; I will not give sleep to my eyes . . . until I find a place for the LORD" (Ps 132:3–5).

Building the House

*Whatever good things we build
end up building us.*
Jim Rohn

Some years ago at the Eucharistic Congress in Dublin, I recall Cardinal Napier recounting that on his arrival at the hotel where we were staying, the concierge who greeted him and took charge of his case said to him, "Follow me, I'm right behind you!" In a way it captures something of the spirituality of St Patrick, whose prayer speaks of God being above and below, before and after and on our every side. Our Father is always at our side.

"When you pray, go into your room and close the door and pray to your Father who is in secret; and your Father who sees in secret will reward you." (Mt 6:6)

Earlier, we considered our Lord's invitation "when you pray, enter . . ." The cultivation of prayer demands discipline, and this action of entering is an important element in that. Resuming that same passage from Matthew's Gospel, let us consider the next phrase in that invitation, to "close the door and pray . . ." This simple Gospel imperative is key in the art of cultivating prayer. When entering into prayer, we need also to close the door, and that is a personal action and an important decision. The way to what is truly in our heart begins by withdrawing from seeking or finding approval in the world around us. For as Jesus says, "Where your treasure is, there will your heart be also" (Lk 12:34).

The passages that come immediately before this section of the Gospel are all about 'being seen', 'parading in public', 'standing ostentatiously in the synagogues and at street corners' – the allure of theatrical gestures, the need to be accepted, respected, thought of as special or superior. It mirrors a certain contemporary thirst for celebrity. As St John Chrysostom puts it, the hypocrites' reward comes from those from whom they most desire to receive it! We must leave behind all the false exteriority of certain Pharisees encountered in the Gospels – the utopias that we can all create for ourselves – leave them outside, and, when it is required of us, close the door on those things for good. "I will not give sleep to my eyes or slumber to my eyelids, until I find a place for the LORD" (Ps 132:4–5).

Jesus also shares this intimate longing. He says: "I want them to be with me where I am" (Jn 17:24). God wishes us to have the faith to trust him: "Leave your own country and go to a land that I will show you" (Gen 12:1). Prayer, in fact, is the most important key to closing the door on sin. Julian of Norwich, the fourteenth-century mystic, had this to say:

> The Lord recalled to my mind the longing I had for him before, and I saw that nothing held me back [in realising this longing] except sin. And so I saw that this is the same for all of us, and thought that if sin had not existed, we would all be as clean and as like to our Lord as he had made us. And thus in my previous folly I had often wondered why, by the great foresighted wisdom of God, the beginning of sin had not been prevented, for then, so I thought, all would have been well. . . . But Jesus . . . said: "Sin is necessary now [by this the Lord is not saying that you have to sin, but that it's a fact with which we have to contend], but all shall be well, and all shall be well, and all manner of things shall be well."

The entire economy of salvation is encompassed between the call of Abraham and the invitation of Jesus. "Leave your native country" on the one hand and then, on the other, "enter your room". The Greek for room is *tameion*, and its first meaning is "treasury".

'Leave and enter'. This actually picks up on the twenty-sixth chapter of Isaiah where we read:

Come, my people, enter your chambers, and shut your doors behind you; hide yourselves for a little while until [my] fury has passed by. (Is 26:20)

The phrases in Isaiah of "enter your chamber" and "shut the door" and "hide yourself", combined with Matthew's "your Father who sees in secret", are parallel to the Gospel passage, but the words of Jesus are more personal. He replaces the prospect of the Lord's fury for the people's wickedness with a gentle invitation instead – not to hide but to be seen by the Father in secret – to enter into the light of God's face, leaving the darkness outside.

I often think of Adoration in the presence of the Blessed Sacrament as a force that gradually begins to purify us interiorly, whose presence begins to refashion the waywardness of our hearts. A force whose effectiveness steadily diminishes the cancerous sinfulness within us. There are, I believe, many testimonies to this. Adoration of the Blessed Sacrament is so important. There is nothing contrary here between entering your room and closing the door and being found at the time of Adoration in a public place. Such an interpretation would be utterly fundamentalist or, at the very least, a lame excuse for avoiding prayer altogether. The verb "to adore" ultimately stems from the verb "to mouth". *Ab ore, ad os* – mouth to mouth – suggests breathing in the same breath of the Spirit which comes from the mouth of Christ, from the vital lungs of his own being. It is the phrase used by God of his encounter with Moses.

In an Epiphany homily, Pope Francis speaks eloquently about this action of adoration:

> Faith demands adoration. If we can fall on our knees before Jesus, we will overcome the temptation to set off on our own path. For adoration involves making an exodus from the greatest form of bondage: slavery to oneself. Adoration means putting the Lord at the centre, not ourselves. It means giving things their rightful place, and giving the first place to God. Adoration means making God's plan more important than our personal time, our entitlements and our spaces. . . . It means being able to speak to him freely and intimately. . . . Adoration means going to Jesus without a list of petitions, but with one request alone: to abide with him. . . . In adoration, we allow Jesus to heal and change us. In adoration, we make it possible for the Lord to transform us by his love, to kindle light amid our darkness, to grant us strength in weakness and courage amid trials. Adoration means concentrating on what is essential: ridding ourselves of useless things and addictions that anaesthetize the heart and confound the mind. In adoration, we learn to reject what should not be adored: the god of money, the god of consumerism, the god of pleasure, the god of success, the god

of self. Adoration means bending low before the Most High and to discover in his presence that life's greatness does not consist in having, but in loving.

"Close the door" clearly implies an action, an asceticism that is needed for prayer; a self-discipline that is required in order that our longing may bear fruit. "Close" – something has to be left behind. Other things and distractions have to be closed out. There are many doors throughout our lives that we must shut as we continue to make progress towards a deeper and more committed interiority. One door we must shut, in one sense, is the door of our senses.

> But I am like a deaf man. I do not hear, like a dumb man who does not open his mouth. Yes, I am like a man who does not hear, and in whose mouth are no rebukes. (Ps 38:13–14)

But there is a counterpart to this that comes about precisely through prayer, for we also hear the prophet say:

> The eyes of the blind shall be opened, and the ears of the deaf unstopped; then shall the lame man leap like a deer, and the tongue of the dumb sing for joy. (Is 35:5–6)

The opening up to a new reality is dependent upon the closing down to another.

Prayer is never simply a matter of what we do. The only thing we can give God is our time. This is the moment in which I choose to be available only for God, who sees me as I am, in my nakedness, without the 'fig leaves', who sees my poverty, who knows what needs to be brought back to life within me, who loves me like no one else and who is there to help me, if not, in fact, to pick me up and carry me all the way.

We have considered how God spoke to Moses saying, "There I will meet you", and how it was noted by the author that it was there that "the Lord spoke to Moses face to face as a man speaks to his friend" (Ex 33:11). Subsequently, we learn in the book of Numbers that when those closest to Moses are criticising him, God in contrast tells them that he considers Moses to be "the most humble of men, the humblest man on earth." Why? Because this is a man of humble prayer. God explains, "If any man among you is a prophet I make myself known to him in a vision, I speak to him in a dream. Not so with my servant Moses: he is at home in my house; I speak with him mouth to mouth, plainly and not in riddles, and he sees the form of the Lord" (Nb 12:3, 6–8). The life of Moses was so deeply prayerful that he was 'at home' with the Lord. What a wonderful, indeed remarkable, picture of intimacy. What immense confidence the Lord showed towards this servant of his – who reciprocated this trust by a life of deep faith.

The words "enter" and "close the door" intensify the sense of interiority, which is what the Lord intends.

We are closed into a small space, a secret space within – the monastic cell, if you like – where no one can enter unless we allow them to do so; and our Father sees us there in this secret and sacred place. The place is finite, circumscribed, enclosed – yet, at the same time, it opens up to the Infinite.

Doors, of course, are very important. They are functional, although some, it is true, are more than merely practical – their grandeur speaks to us. We only have to think of the great and solemn, beautiful doors to the basilicas in Rome – doors to which artists have given a soul.

We could usefully develop a simple phenomenological meditation on the door. It gives onto space; it allows the movement from one place to another; there is its exterior side and its more mysterious interior side. By passing through it, we go from one reality to another. How very poignant is the prison gate that opens to release a prisoner into freedom. Perhaps most significantly, a door is an expression of free will, of a decision to open or to close. A wall, on the other hand, is utterly "totalitarian": there is no going through it – unless, of course, you are the Risen Lord! Jesus' instruction teaches us that we must *decide* to pray as well as long to pray. His "Let what you say be simply Yes or No; anything more than this comes from the evil one" (Mt 5:37) might also be understood to mean, a door needs to be either open or closed!

Throughout Scripture there are many strong symbolic senses of doors and passages. The first one, of course, is of being shut out after the fall from paradise, whose entrance is now guarded by cherubim and the flaming, ever-turning sword (Gen 3:23–24). In Matthew 6, the Lord invites us through prayer to come back via that same door that has shut us out on account of our sin. Prayer can be seen as the antidote to our original expulsion from paradise, the gradual cleansing of our sinful and stubborn selves. By responding to Jesus' invitation, we walk past the cherubim and the flaming sword that "turned in all directions" and re-enter paradise to walk again and talk again with God "in the cool of the evening" (Gen 3:8). What a wonderful image of prayer! The door which Jesus asks us to close in prayer shuts us within paradise.

Jesus himself, of course, often speaks of doors and uses them as symbols in his parables and elsewhere. Indeed, he claims to be the only door. "If anyone enters by me, he will be saved and will go in and out and find pasture" (Jn 10:9).

In another section of the Sermon on the Mount, we hear him say, "Enter through the narrow door . . ." (Mt 7:13–14). Now, we know that with Jesus there is nothing grand or enormous – that will only come with his appearing at the end of time when we shall see him in all his majesty, in all his glory. Here, he speaks of a humble, narrow door – a modest, narrow way – one that is not cluttered – one that befits the beggar who has nothing yet who seeks everything. There is no alternative but to enter, "for the Kingdom of God is within" (Lk 17:21).

It is in this room that we are invited to pray to our Father in secret. It is here that Jesus teaches us not to heap up empty phrases and instead gives us the words of the "Our Father" which tell us that Jesus is also present in the room with us. In John's thinking, he is there to ensure our good pasture (see Jn 10:9). He does not abandon us to ourselves. He bequeaths to us his own intimate relationship with the Father. It is "no longer I, but Christ who lives in me" (Gal 2:20). Authentic Christian prayer begins when I realise that Christ is praying in me. This is the "in secret" of which Jesus speaks. "For it is not you who speak, but the Spirit of your Father speaking through you" (Mt 10:20). "God has sent the Spirit of his Son into our hearts, crying, 'Abba! Father!'" (Gal 4:6). "Likewise the Spirit helps us in our weakness; for we do not know how to pray as we ought, but the Spirit himself intercedes for us with sighs too deep for words . . . for the Spirit intercedes for the saints according to the will of God" (Rm 8:26–27).

Abbot Jeremy Driscoll, OSB, in his book *What Happens at Mass*, writes, when commenting on the Our Father:

> When Jesus teaches us the name "Father" for our most intimate address to God – in imitation of his own – we have just one more instance of the miracle

of Christ's incarnation, the miracle in which finite, limited forms are made capable of bearing infinite divine realities. The finite, limited form – in this case the name "Father" – bends under the weight of the divine reality it carries and is re-defined beyond its limitations. . . . But in the mouth of the eternal Word become flesh, "Father" is the finite, limited name he gave us, which is a gate through which we pass into an infinite reality; namely, his own loving relation to the Source from which he himself is eternally begotten.

In the book of Revelation, we hear the Lord say: "Behold, I stand at the door and knock" (Rv 3:20). Here, he is outside, humbly knocking on our door, asking us to let him in. Paul Claudel reminds us that most people say 'no' to this invitation and refuse to open the door. He writes:

What is meant if not that lost door in the basement of our soul. . . . We are like a bad tenant allowed to remain through charity in a house that does not belong to him, that he has neither built nor paid for, and who barricades himself and refuses to receive the rightful owner even for a minute. . . . It is such a nuisance to get up and open that old door! It is fastened by two bolts that sum up all that is inert and immovable: one is called 'bad habits' and the other 'ill will'. As for the lock, that is our own secret. The key is lost. We would have to get oil to make it turn.

The door, which is Christ, is never barred; all we need to do is unlock it.

There is a story in the life of Houdini, the Hungarian-American illusionist and stunt performer who was particularly famous for his spectacular escape acts. His biography relates that the lock which foxed him most was the one that the locksmith had purposefully left open and which Houdini, in trying to open it, had in fact locked!

"Knock and the door will be opened" (Lk 11:9) is the promise that is made to us by the Lord who remains true to his word. A prayer which opens the Season of Advent captures this well:

> Keep us alert, we pray, O Lord our God,
> as we await the advent of Christ your Son,
> so that, when he comes and knocks,
> he may find us watchful in prayer
> and exultant in his praise.

The Garden of Sin

Saruman is plotting to become a Power!
J.R.R. Tolkien

A story is told of an old man who was driving his car along the motorway. He noticed that a police car began to follow him, so he accelerated away at high speed. The police car put on its lights and sounded its claxon. Eventually the old man pulled into the side. "I'm too old for this", he said to himself. The policeman approached, looked at him and said, "I'm off duty in ten minutes. If you can give me a good reason why you were speeding, I'll let you go." "Well", the old man said, "twenty years ago my wife ran off with another man. He was a police-man. And I thought he was bringing her back!"

I suspect we all recognise something familiar about this tale. It is certainly reminiscent of Adam's excuse in the Garden of Eden, which through man's choice turned into a garden of sin. Sin can so often be dressed up in comfortable excuses, not simply for not saying things as they are but allowing our own thinking to diminish or excuse the sinfulness of what we do or say or neglect – that little voice that finds a plausible excuse for what we have done or not done, or said or not said. We are all prone to self-deception.

When General Eisenhower liberated the concentration camps at the end of the Second World War, he ordered every available photographer and cinematographer to enter the camps and photograph everything exactly as they found it. He also arranged for civilians from outside to be taken into the camps because he feared that down the road of history some would say this never happened. How true that has proved to be! The same can be said today of sin. Many live in denial of it and of its venomous nature. This infestation in the garden, not simply of weeds but of something that attacks even the healthy plants at their root, needs careful attention.

The book of Wisdom cautions us against a disregard for sin:

> God made man imperishable, he made him in the image of his own nature; it was the devil's envy that brought death into the world, as those who are his partners will discover. But the souls of the virtuous are in the hands of God. (Wis 2:23–3:1)

Like Adam and Eve, we also experience the subtle deceptions of temptation, which the serpent used to allure our first parents into sin. The Fathers of the Church speak of the serpent as originally being the most friendly and congenial of animals towards our first parents and say that Satan used this charm, out of envy, to deceive and trap them.

At Mass each day, we pray, "Look not on our sins, but on the faith of your Church." Faith is opposite to sin. This speaks to us about an important orientation in our Christian discipleship. In what direction are we facing? To whom is our life aligned? To whom do we belong, to the Lord or to ourselves? Lack of faith, a lack of trust in God, taking ourselves too seriously – the self-idolatry to which we are all prone – is the root that can run deep in our heart and in our exercise of free will. Our first parents were not looking to God when they sinned but to themselves, and this they did knowingly. The book of Genesis tells us that God made man the ruler over all creation, yet he freely stooped to trust the voice of the serpent, who was subject to man, rather than the voice of God, who had created him (Gen 3:4–5).

The book of Wisdom again muses on this folly:

> For all men who were ignorant of God were foolish by nature; and they were unable from the good things that are seen to know him who exists, nor did they recognize the craftsman while paying heed to his works. . . . If through delight in the beauty of these things men assumed them to be gods, let them know how much better than these is their Lord, for the author of beauty created them. (Wis 13:1, 3)

When Pope Francis visited the people of Tacloban in the Philippines in 2015, their lives had been shattered just over a year before by Typhoon Yolanda. He said to them as he pointed to the crucifix:

> We have a high priest who is capable of sympathising with our weaknesses. . . . Jesus is like us. Jesus lived like us and is the same as us in every respect, except sin because he was not a sinner. But in order to be more like us he assumed our condition and our sin. He made himself into sin! This is what St Paul tells us. Jesus always goes before us and when we pass through an experience, a cross, he has passed there before us. And if today we find ourselves [after these terrible experiences], it is because we have the security of knowing we will not weaken in our faith because Jesus has been here before us. In his Passion he assumed all our pain.

The natural devastation suffered during that disaster might well serve for us as an image of the hidden effects of personal sinfulness in our own lives and in the life of the Church, and of the desperate need we have to be revived in hope and to be anointed by mercy.

The Holy Father had spoken about this earlier in *Evangelii Gaudium*, where he speaks about the power of intercessory prayer:

The great men and women of God were great inter-cessors. Intercession is like a "leaven" in the heart of the Trinity. It is a way of penetrating the Father's heart and discovering new dimensions which can shed light on concrete situations and change them. We can say that God's heart is touched by our intercession, yet in reality he is always there first.

The idea that the Lord "is always there first" combined with the sense that intercessory prayer is a like "a 'leaven' in the heart of the Trinity" that is capable of "penetrating the Father's heart" could serve us well as we prepare to confess our sins.

The idea that the Lord is ahead of us should not surprise us, but it should help us to understand better the reality of God's closeness to us even in our sinfulness and of his concern for us especially in the sacrament of Penance, which offers to exchange sterile soil for that which is fertile. In reality, the Lord waits unwearyingly for the sinner. This is an image captured by Jesus himself, as he sat jadedly by the well waiting for the woman of Samaria (Jn 4:1–42). The great sequence *Dies irae* captures this beautifully:

Quaerens me sedisti lassus,	In search of me you sat down weary;
Redemisti crucem passus:	you redeemed me by suffering the Cross.

Tantus labor non sit cassus.   May so great a labour
                                  not be in vain.

In the previous stanza, "*Recordare, Iesu pie*", the poet reminds us that the infinite mercy of God is expressed by the warmth of Jesus' affection. He tells us that we are the reason for his journey on this earth, and he pleads that we may not be lost on "*illa die*" – that fateful day!

The modern version of the Church's ancient discipline of public penance is the queue of penitents outside the confessional. It is a statement to everyone that I am a sinner awaiting absolution and reconciliation with the Church. How would people react if they discovered Jesus in that queue? Some would drag him out! The priest hearing confessions might say to him, like John the Baptist, "I have need to be absolved by you and do you come to me?" I rather suspect, however, that Jesus would be unperturbed by those who are scandalised and would stay put! "For our sake he made him to be sin who knew no sin, so that in him we might become the righteousness of God" (2 Cor 5:21).

What a wonderful image for us to have in our minds as we approach the confessional. How encouraging, even sometimes in our own tiredness as we administer the sacraments, to know that we share that same weariness with the Lord who is there in the confessional even before we enter it and is also waiting for us in the queue outside. We do nothing without him; we should endeavour to become conscious of the fact that we experience nothing without him either. The Lord is the one who waits patiently, longingly, lovingly for the sinner, even when tired.

Let us keep in mind the garden in Eden. At the fall, God "drove out the man, and at the east of the garden of Eden he placed the cherubim, and a flaming sword that turned every way, to guard the way to the tree of life" (Gen 3:24). Sin drives us out, away, puts us into the cold, into an arid and desolate wasteland. In the sacrament of Penance our baptismal grace is restored and we are led back towards paradise. The flaming sword which is wielded in every direction to prevent us returning to the source of life is replaced by the two-edged sword of God's word which "discerns all the thoughts and intentions of our hearts" (Heb 4:12) and which is spoken sacramentally in the confessional. The tree of life, the *lignum vitae*, is the cross of Christ himself who, far from barring the way to paradise, leads us back to the source of life using the cross itself as a plank, a bridge across which to draw us to himself (see Jn 12:32). Far from being a gatekeeper, a bishop or priest, as cultivator, undertakes more the role of the usher: welcoming, walking alongside, enabling the sinner "through the ministry of the Church" to find the way to the very source of eternal life.

The Holy Doors in Rome and throughout the Catholic world, which were flung open during the Jubilee Year of Mercy with great and joyous ceremony, could very well serve as an appropriate image for the heart of bishops and priests who are ordained to serve as ministers of mercy and who are given the power to forgive sins as the Lord commanded. It is as if the Lord says to us in our ministry: "To you all flesh will come with its burden of sin. Too heavy for us, our offences, but you wipe them away" (Ps 65:3b–4).

God does not hide. We hear his footsteps, as Adam and Eve did, but they are the footsteps of a Father who doesn't wait indifferently for the return of his child, but who on seeing him afar off spontaneously runs towards him out of an overwhelming love for the boy, wishing only to embrace his child and to restore him to life. This generosity surprises the son as much as it does the servants of the house, and the elder son, more judgemental than merciful, is deeply scandalised by his merciful father (Lk 15:11–32)!

All of us are aware of our deep poverty as we stand before the sacrament of Penance, the Holy Door of Mercy. There we know we stand before Christ himself, who knows our deep poverty, our guilt, our need for mercy, for healing, for the Father's compassionate embrace. As we come to understand this, it is then that as bishops and priests, who are first of all sinners, that our gaze becomes his gaze, our attitude his attitude, our welcoming his welcome as we enfold each penitent in this mystery of divine love.

One of the panels on the Holy Door in St Peter's Basilica depicts a shepherd who clings precariously with his left hand to the edge of a precipice while strenuously stretching with his right hand to grasp the fallen sheep on an inaccessible ledge below. It is an icon of the profound nature of God's love. It is an icon too of a bishop and priest – the shepherd who risks everything for the life of the stray sheep.

Pope Francis never tires of challenging us to allow ourselves to 'be mercied'. It is there in his episcopal motto *miserando atque eligendo*. The use of the gerund is important because it emphasises an act and serves as an antidote to those who say that all this talk of mercy is superficial. No, 'mercying' – *miserando* – speaks to us of a divine action, and, furthermore, in being 'mercied' ourselves we also become the protagonists of mercy. We are caught up in a theandric dynamic whereby we receive something that is proper to God's own nature – his mercy. In the memorable phrase of Pope Francis, the sacrament of Penance is a true fountain of mercy and not a "torture chamber"!

St Augustine in his *Confessions*, addressing the Father, encourages us with a sense of hope:

> There is good reason for my solid hope in him, because you will heal all my infirmities through him who sits at your right hand and intercedes for us. Were it not so, I should despair; for many and grave are those infirmities, many and grave; but wider-reaching is your healing power. We might have despaired of ourselves, thinking your Word remote from any conjunction with mankind, had he not become flesh and made his dwelling among us. Filled with terror by my sins and my load of misery,

I had been turning over in my mind a plan to flee into solitude; but you forbade me, and strengthened me by your words: To this end Christ died for all, that they who are alive might live not for themselves but for him who died for them. See, then, Lord: I cast my care upon you so that I may live, and I will contemplate the wonders you have revealed. You know how stupid and weak I am: teach me and heal me. Your only Son, in whom are hidden all treasures of wisdom and knowledge, has redeemed me with his blood. Let not the proud disparage me, for I am mindful of my ransom. I eat it, I drink it, I dispense it to others, and as a poor man I long to be filled with it among those who are fed and feasted. And then, let those who seek him praise the Lord.

The words of the Roman poet Terence, "*Homo sum, humani nil a me alienum puto!*" can equally be applied to Jesus – I am a man, and I consider myself no alien to anything human! As St Paul says, "For our sake he made him to be sin who knew no sin, so that in him we might become the righteousness of God" (2 Cor 5:21). The phrase "to be sin" is a reference by Paul to the book of Leviticus, chapter 4. There, the Hebrew and Greek Old Testaments simply use the word 'sin' to mean 'sin offering'. The expiatory sacrifice for sin is called, quite simply, 'sin', thus bringing together Paul's startling assertion that Jesus was made "to be sin who knew no sin." The sacrifice on the cross is the fulfilment of all ancient sacrifices.

It is important to look at this garden with honesty and then to set to work. Indeed, in it we find a lifetime's work. The devil's tactic in the face of such a long project is to sow despondency, which in reality is another form of pride. If we realised how original sin has so deeply affected us, we should not be surprised at our constant need to uproot the weeds and to acknowledge that were it not for God's grace we would have fallen still lower and more often. As the Psalm so beautifully puts it, "You care for the earth, give it water, you fill it with riches. Your river in heaven brims over to provide its grain. And thus you provide for the earth; you drench its furrows; you level it, soften it with showers; you bless its growth" (Ps 65:10–11). God brings about a new fragrance through his action of mercy, which awakens us once more to life and offers us peace and a safe arbour under which to rest.

We would do well to pay attention to Chesterton's cautionary note: "It is not always wrong even to go, like Dante, to the brink of the lowest promontory and look down at hell. It is when you look up at hell that a serious miscalculation has probably been made."

The Garden of Suffering

Courage is almost a contradiction in terms.
It means a strong desire to live taking the form
of a readiness to die.
G.K. Chesterton

There are two scenes from the Gospels of Matthew and Luke that are worth placing together in order to reflect on the next garden.

The first, from Luke, follows Jesus' first prediction of his Passion and of his disciple's need to follow him by taking up their own crosses:

About eight days after Jesus said this, he took Peter, John and James with him and went up onto a mountain to pray. As he was praying, the appearance of his face changed, and his clothes became as bright as a flash of lightning. Two men, Moses and Elijah, appeared in glorious splendour, talking with Jesus. They spoke about his departure, which he was about to bring to fulfilment at Jerusalem. Peter and his companions were very sleepy, but when they became fully awake, they saw his glory and the two men standing with him. As the men were leaving Jesus, Peter said to him, "Master, it is good for us to be here. Let us put up three shelters – one for you, one for Moses and one for Elijah." (He did not know what he was saying.) While he was speaking, a cloud appeared and covered them, and they were afraid as they entered the cloud. A voice came from the cloud, saying, "This is my Son, whom I have chosen; listen to him." When the voice had spoken, they found that Jesus was alone. The disciples kept this to themselves and did not tell anyone what they had seen. (Lk 9:28–36)

Then, from Matthew:

Jesus went with them to a place called Gethsemane, and he said to his disciples, "Sit here, while I go over there and pray." And taking with him Peter and the two sons of Zebedee, he began to be sorrowful and troubled. Then he said to them, "My soul is overwhelmed with sorrow to the point of death; remain here, and watch with me." And going a little farther he fell on his face and prayed, saying, "My Father, if it is possible, may this cup be taken from me. Yet not as I will, but as you will." And he came to the disciples and found them sleeping. And he said to Peter, "So, could you not watch with me one hour? Watch and pray that you may not enter into temptation. The spirit indeed is willing, but the flesh is weak." Again, for the second time, he went away and prayed, "My Father, if this cannot pass unless I drink it, your will be done." And again he came and found them sleeping, for their eyes were heavy. So, leaving them again, he went away and prayed for the third time, saying the same words again. Then he came to the disciples and said to them, "Sleep and take your rest later on. See, the hour is at hand, and the Son of Man is betrayed into the hands of sinners. Rise, let us be going; see, my betrayer is at hand." While he was still speaking, Judas came, one of the twelve, and with him a great crowd with swords and clubs, from the chief priests and the elders of the people. Now the betrayer had given them a sign, saying, "The one I will kiss is the man; seize him." And he came up to Jesus at once and said, "Greetings, Rabbi!" And he kissed him. Jesus said to him, "Friend, do what you came to do." Then they came up and laid hands on Jesus and seized him and behold, one of those who were with Jesus stretched out his hand and drew his sword and struck the servant of the high priest and cut off his ear. Then Jesus said to him, "Put your sword back into its place. For all who take the sword will perish by the sword. Do you think that I cannot appeal to my Father, and he will at once send me more than twelve legions of angels? But how then should the Scriptures be fulfilled, that it must be so?" At that hour Jesus said to the crowds, "Have you come out as against a robber, with swords and clubs to capture me? Day after day I sat in the temple teaching, and you did not seize me. But all this has taken place that the Scriptures of the prophets might be fulfilled." Then all the disciples left him and fled. (Mt 26:36–56)

The similarities and contrasts between these accounts are considerable. The protagonists are the same in both: Jesus, Peter, James and John. The other Apostles are left either at the foot of the mountain or outside the garden gate. In both scenes, Jesus goes to pray; in both, the disciples fall asleep. There is a contrast between light and darkness. On the mountain the glory of Jesus is revealed; in the garden the depth of his humanity in his overwhelming sorrow. One speaks of life, the other of death. While on the one hand, Moses and Elijah come to talk with Jesus on Tabor, their presence consoles the disciples who are devastated by Jesus' announcement of his death and the conditions of discipleship; while, in Gethsemane, an angel comes to comfort and strengthen Jesus himself (Lk 22:43). In both, we discern that despite the presence of others, Jesus nevertheless is alone. While in the first scene Peter is filled with the light-headed enthusiasm of the moment, in the other he struggles to deal with what is happening. In the one, Jesus tells them not to speak of what has happened, and in the other to pray not to fall into temptation. Then in Matthew, the scene develops beyond the similarities into a spiral of betrayal and deceit, violence and rough handling, arrest and abandonment, and the display of cowardice.

Those who live or work with the sick are often the witnesses to some of the most challenging moments in life, facing, as they do, the acute circumstances that are part and parcel of human existence, of suffering and of death. There are moments of deep sadness and tragedy, and moments of immense joy and relief. More often, when faced with serious illness, the things that are most important in life come to the fore, while other things just fade away as insignificant. Illness nearly always brings about a stripping away of the unessential and faces us with raw reality. It can also give birth to a deep fear. Fear presents itself in many ways: panic is an obvious reaction; denial of what's happening another; and for some, the immensity of what they now face prompts them to escape, sometimes by turning or running away, and sometimes by simply being sapped of the little energy they have remaining. Fainting is a good example, but there can also be the onset of a deep lethargy which can confine someone even to their bed for days, or to sleep for much of the time. This is much more common than many realise. It happens, too, on battlefields. Sometimes the most vociferously valiant soldier can, in the face of reality, suddenly lose his heroism.

All fear, of course, is ultimately the fear of death, of annihilation, whether it be a fear in the presence of a wild beast, or an illness, or simply something that brings us face to face with the unknown. This can happen even in the realm of friendships and relationships.

It occurs to me that this was possibly one of the reasons why the three close friends of the Lord fell asleep so readily when Jesus was within hours of his own cruel death. The experience of overpowering sleep is a psychological riddle. Again, as in the garden in Eden, the instinct on hearing the 'footsteps' was to hide. Certainly the experience of this moment detached the Apostles from Jesus. They were not with him at a deep level; and, as is evident, he was not able to rely on them.

It is often very difficult to describe suffering and sorrow. There is something hidden and mysterious about it; something that isolates a person from everything and everyone around them. It can be dehumanising. Jesus himself withdrew into the shadows of the olive trees. They alone witnessed the entire intensity of his agony, which in its crushing grip was yielding a precious oil that would eventually anoint the sufferings and the wounds of many.

We can often complicate life. Complexity, rather like barbed wire, gets in the way, preventing us from crossing with ease from one side to the other without being shredded – unless of course we leap over the obstacle; unless we begin to see the obstacle more simply, as part of a larger perspective, and certainly by not by caving in upon ourselves.

Like the Apostles, we often come either to a high mountain or enter into a garden. Both invite us to be with Jesus and to face with him the reality of the moment – and its significance – and to pray. Eight of the eleven were left at the garden gate, while he passes deeper into the shadows with the three. Peter, James, and John had been witnesses of his prayers before on Tabor. They now experience, although somewhat at a distance, a no less wonderful revelation of his glory in his filial submission to the Father. It was a different 'entering in'. There is something remarkable in Matthew's expression "he began to be sorrowful", as if a sudden wave broke over him and swept everything else aside. A storm of agitation and panic broke his calm, as he uttered, "My soul is overwhelmed with sorrow to the point of death."

While we may not entirely appreciate through our own experiences of life the full drama of what Jesus himself experienced – how could we? – these moments in the garden and on the mountain are of immense significance for us on our own journey, both in light and dark moments, in the ups and the downs of our lives. They tell us that even if we are afraid, or asleep or weak or lacking in courage, it is nevertheless important to remain or enter with Jesus even into the unknowing, the uncomprehending moments. St John Henry Newman wrote somewhere, "This, then, is to watch: to be detached from what is present, and to live in what is unseen."

At the end of the agony in the garden, Jesus returns to his friends. "Sleep and take your rest later on", he says. "See, the hour is at hand, and the Son of Man is betrayed into the hands of sinners. Rise, let us be going; see, my betrayer is at hand" (Mt 26:45–46). After facing his own weakness, perhaps even the thought of not being humanly strong enough to carry the cross or endure all the torture that was to be part of the next day, Jesus in these moments had thrown himself into the mystery of the Father's will: "My Father, if this cannot pass unless I drink it, your will be done." I think this should give us great courage in the face of whatever challenge is before us, whatever our struggle may be. For, when we say 'yes' to the Father's will, when we surrender ourselves to him by acceptance rather than by resignation, he gives us the grace to do it, whatever it is. Jean Pierre de Caussade was to note that the Lord never sends anything to us that isn't good for our soul.

Pope St Leo the Great, when reflecting upon the redemptive act of Christ, puts into antithesis the words 'exemplum' and 'mysterium' or 'sacramentum'. The 'mystery' is something into which we enter and which is greater than we are. It is something that never fails to yield a harvest. An 'example', on the other hand, is simply an illustration of what is humanly possible. Mystery has a relational element to it. It places our inadequacy and weakness into a context which is greater and which gives to us possibility. If all one gets from prayer is the devastating truth of one's sinfulness, then it is not of God for, above all, he brings us grace. The challenge is then to accept the grace which gives us the courage to say 'yes' and the wherewithal to face life. The Lord himself reminds us: "My grace is sufficient for you, for My power is perfected in weakness" (2 Cor 12:9).

Etty Hillesum, a Jewish woman who died in Auschwitz at the age of twenty-nine, had lived what we might call a very colourful life. She was highly intelligent and an atheist, that is, until she passionately fell in love with God whom she discovered through suffering in unimaginable circumstances. Amazingly, she describes her initial months in the concentration camp as "the two richest and most intense months of my life, in which my highest values were so deeply confirmed. I have learned to love Westerbork." She realised how dehumanising suffering can be, but that by turning away from the dark hollow of distress in order to find something of a higher value, namely God, we can also live with courage in the midst of disaster. She wrote in her diary: "When I say, I have come to terms with life, I don't mean I have lost hope. . . . It is a question of living life from minute to minute and taking suffering into the bargain. And it is certainly no small bargain these days. . . . But I know that . . . somewhere there is something inside me that will never desert me again."

The terrifying footsteps of the SS officers, the inhuman conditions that prevailed within the camps, did not rob her of the greater discovery that she had now come to realise. St Paul reflects upon this too when writing about the law of the Spirit of life in Christ:

If God is for us, who can ever be against us? Since he did not spare even his own Son but gave him up for us all, won't he also give us everything else? Who dares accuse us whom God has chosen for his own? No one—for God himself has given us right standing with himself. Who then will condemn us? No one—for Christ Jesus died for us and was raised to life for us, and he is sitting in the place of honour at God's right hand, pleading for us. Can anything ever separate us from Christ's love? Does it mean he no longer loves us if we have trouble or calamity, or are persecuted, or hungry, or destitute, or in danger, or threatened with death? (As the Scriptures say, "For your sake we are killed every day; we are being slaughtered like sheep.") No, despite all these things, overwhelming victory is ours through Christ, who loved us. And I am convinced that nothing can ever separate us from God's love. Neither death nor life, neither angels nor demons, neither our fears for today nor our worries about tomorrow – not even the powers of hell can separate us from God's love. No power in the sky above or in the earth below – indeed, nothing in all creation will ever be able to separate us from the love of God that is revealed in Christ Jesus our Lord. (Rm 8:31–39)

We are inadequate before the great mystery of God. How could we be otherwise? We were made for greatness, and when suffering comes along we become very small under its spell. St Luke records:

> Then he said to them all: "Whoever wants to be my disciple must deny themselves and take up their cross daily and follow me. For whoever wants to save their life will lose it, but whoever loses their life for me will save it. What good is it for someone to gain the whole world, and yet lose or forfeit their very self? Whoever is ashamed of me and my words, the Son of Man will be ashamed of them when he comes in his glory and in the glory of the Father and of the holy angels." . . . While they were all marvelling at everything he was doing, Jesus said to his disciples, "You put these words of mine into your ears: The Son of Man is about to be delivered into the hands of men." But they did not understand this saying, and it was concealed from them, so that they might not perceive it. And they were afraid to ask him about this saying. An argument arose among them as to which of them was the greatest. But Jesus, knowing the reasoning of their hearts, took a child and put him by his side and said to them, "Whoever receives this child in my name receives me, and whoever receives me receives him who sent me. For he who is least among you all is the one who is great." (Lk 9:23–26, 43–48)

The announcement of the Passion and the teaching about discipleship just hadn't sunk in. To be a little child! That is how the Lord looks on us – little children, naughty, sinful, sometimes cowardly and unwise perhaps. But one day when we have gone through this valley of tears and have been scarred by so many things, yet have remained committed to being faithful, the Father will hold us in his arms and see something of the same wounds on us that are on the body of his own Son. That will be the identity card that allows us to pass from this garden of suffering to a much safer place. "Truly I have set my soul in tranquillity and silence. Like a weaned child on its mother; like a weaned child is my soul within me" (Ps 131:2).

The Garden of Victory

There is something sadder to lose than life –
the reason for living;
Sadder than to lose one's possessions is to lose one's hope.
Paul Claudel

Charles Dickens, in *A Christmas Carol*, says of Ebenezer Scrooge, who was awaiting the next ghostly revelation to appear, "Being prepared for almost anything, he was not by any means prepared for nothing"!

The surprise that met Mary Magdalene certainly seems to have been beyond her anticipation.

Now on the first day of the week Mary Magdalene came to the tomb early, while it was still dark, and saw that the stone had been taken away from the tomb. So she ran and went to Simon Peter and the other disciple, the one whom Jesus loved, and said to them, "They have taken the Lord out of the tomb, and we do not know where they have laid him." So

Peter went out with the other disciple, and they were going toward the tomb. Both of them were running together, but the other disciple outran Peter and reached the tomb first. And stooping to look in, he saw the linen cloths lying there, but he did not go in. Then Simon Peter came, following him, and went into the tomb. He saw the linen cloths lying there, and the face cloth, which had been on Jesus' head, not lying with the linen cloths but folded up in a place by itself. Then the other disciple, who had reached the tomb first, also went in, and he saw and believed; for as yet they did not understand the Scripture, that he must rise from the dead. (Jn 20:1–9)

St Gregory the Great says the fact that "it was still dark" indicates to us the state of Mary's faith at this moment, as well as that of the other disciples. Romanus, on the other hand, in his commentary suggests that the faith of the women was stronger than that of the other disciples. The great Kontakion on the Resurrection expresses it this way: "The young women bearing incense hasten towards the dawn, as though seeking day! . . . The wise women . . . sent forward Mary Magdalene. . . . It was dark, but love lighted the way for her."

We come face to face at this moment in the Gospels with the inevitability of death, which of itself, of its nature, in its consequences, offers nothing to sustain an understanding of anything beyond it. It is God's

Spirit alone that gives us an intuition that death is not our natural and final state. Yet the drama in this garden tells us that the first followers of Jesus were facing the reality of failure and of annihilation in its starkest form.

We get a further glimpse of this in Luke's account of the two disciples who were on the road to Emmaus after the Crucifixion. Eusebius has it that Cleopas in this account is "Cleopas, the brother of St Joseph", which, if it were so, would make him the uncle of Jesus, which emphasises even more for us how surprising this encounter was.

> They were talking with each other about all these things that had happened. While they were talking and discussing together, Jesus himself drew near and went with them. But their eyes were kept from recognising him. And he said to them, "What is this conversation that you are holding with each other as you walk?" And they stood still, looking sad. (Lk 24:14–17)

We owe St Luke a great deal for his observations as a physician. It is very easy to 'stand still', to wallow in self-pity, to stay in Gethsemane, to be incapable of seeing beyond what is so evidently tragic, of comprehending that moment as we idle like an old tractor on its last legs hiccupping in the throes of collapse.

"Are you the only visitor to Jerusalem who does not know the things that have happened there in these days?" And he said to them, "What things?" [They were aghast that he didn't know.] And they said to him, "Concerning Jesus of Nazareth, a man who was a prophet mighty in deed and word before God and all the people. . . . We had hoped that he was the one to redeem Israel." (Lk 24:18–19, 21)

Viktor Frankl (1905–1997), Professor of Neurology and Psychiatry in the University of Vienna and the founder of the Third Viennese School of Psychotherapy (the first being Freud's psychoanalysis, and the second Adler's individual psychology), established his theory of Logotherapy following his experience as a prisoner and survivor of Auschwitz. In his book *Man's Search for Meaning*, he tells us how he began to realise that his fellow prisoners started to waste away and die because they had lost the motivation to live and had buckled under the darkness of this tragic moment. Frankl began to pick up 'meanings' in their personal stories and very gently began to feed these 'meanings' back to them. What he noticed, much to his surprise, was that as he did so, his companions who had practically given up were suddenly encouraged again and, in finding a meaning for life, began to cope with the torture and the hardships of the camp. We understand, of course, the Christian significance of Logos, which we translate as 'Word', but its primary signification is 'meaning'!

Hermann Hesse, the German-born Swiss Evangelical poet, novelist, and painter of the last century, makes this apposite observation:

> Every man goes through this period of crisis. For the average man it is the point in his life when the demands of his own fate are at odds with his environment, when the way ahead is most hardly won. For many it is the only time that they experience the dying and resurrection which is our lot, during the decay and slow collapse of childhood when we are abandoned by everything we love, and suddenly feel the loneliness and deathly cold of the world around us. And a great many people stay forever hanging on to this cliff and cling desperately their whole life through to the irrevocable past, the dream of the lost paradise which is the worst and most ruthless of all dreams.

To have the hope that is beyond the finality of death, something else, entirely gratuitous, needs to enter a moment such as this. Our spirit has to be rooted in and search out something that transcends the historicity of this final point. Failure in one form or another is our common lot. It is certainly more common than hope, for while everyone dies, not everyone lives with an expectation of something more. Living without an eye to faith leaves us prey to a form of self-idolatry.

In the book of Numbers there is a cautionary tale (Nb 11). It recounts how the Israelites complained about the manna God had given to them in the desert. They wanted more. They wanted meat. When God gave them what they wanted, some were so greedy that they died of their gluttony and were buried in *Kibroth Hattaavah*, which means the 'Graves of Craving'. It serves as a powerful metaphor for self-destruction following upon the self-fulfilment that is self-idolatry. Self-gratification, self-indulgence, self-satisfaction, self-referencing – the abandonment of ourselves to our cravings can become a way of life that is ultimately the way to the death of the spirit which the Old Testament expresses in terms of 'forgetting God': "But they soon forgot his works, they did not wait for his counsel. They had a wonton craving in the wilderness and put God to the test in the desert" (Ps 106:13–14). The Graves of Craving symbolise the destiny that awaits those who do not believe that God will take care of them, will sustain them in every circumstance of life.

In Etty Hillesum's diary entry for 20 July 1942, a year before her own death in the concentration camp, she wrote: "Oh God, times are too hard for frail people like myself. I know that a new and kinder day will come. I would so much like to live on, if only to express all the love that I carry within me. And there is only one way of preparing the new age, by living it even now in our hearts." She was not thinking at this moment of heaven, but then neither were the Israelites in the desert, but she understood more than they did.

For the two disciples on the road to Emmaus this was a static moment. Historically, Jesus' mission had come to nothing. He had died a failure. Like the prophets before him, he had not accomplished the conversion of his people. In a very real sense he had truly 'lost his own life'. If public approval were to be the criterion of success, then it would be understandable if the disciples were to think in this downcast moment that Barabbas had been more successful than Jesus. They were facing complete bewilderment, disorientation, despair.

They continued their conversation with Jesus:

> "Some of those who were with us went to the tomb and found it just as the women had said, but him they did not see." And he said to them, "O foolish ones, and slow of heart to believe all that the prophets have spoken! Was it not necessary that the Christ should suffer these things and enter into his glory?" And beginning with Moses and all the Prophets, he interpreted to them in all the Scriptures the things concerning himself. (Lk 24:24–27)

St Augustine, contrasting this moment with the scene of Christ dying on the cross alongside the good thief, comments:

They had given up hope. . . . O my dear disciples, you had hoped once, now you do not hope? Come here, Thief, give the disciples a lesson. Why have you given up hope, just because you have seen him crucified, because you have looked at him hanging there, because you have thought him weak? He was like that for the Thief too, hanging on the cross beside him. The Thief was sharing in his punishment but he believed straightaway and acknowledged him, while you on the other hand have forgotten that he is the author of life. Cry out, O Thief, from the cross! You, a criminal, win over the saints! What did they say? "We had hoped that he was the one to redeem Israel". What did this man say? "Jesus, remember me, when you come into your kingdom". So you had hoped, had you, that it was he who would redeem Israel? O my dear disciples, if he was the one who was going to redeem Israel, it means that you have defected. But he has reinstated you; he did not abandon you. By becoming your companion on the way, he himself became for you the way.

The cause of their despair was that they considered him dead. It had literally taken their breath away – that breath of life given to them by the living Christ, the Incarnate Word of God, in what he had shared with them, in what he had taught them and with which in this moment they were not able to reconnect.

When we consider that Jesus bore his cross for the salvation of the world, we are accepting or better understanding that he endured genuine, humiliating, radical failure for the salvation of mankind! It was and remains a turning upside down of the world's assessment of so many things. In contrast to us, Jesus' complete hope in God enabled him to accept history's verdict on the failure of his life and mission. This is not fatalism. It is the recognition that the one who cannot freely lay down his life is the one whose ideals and values are seriously compromised. How often we are all faced with such frustrations.

How quickly we see that this lesson was learnt in Luke-Acts where we see the shift of the mission move from Jerusalem to Rome. This had not been expected, but by this time the early Church had learnt to trust the Lord, to keep its eyes on him and not to worry about its own shortcomings and failures. The cross was the failure. The divine solution, on the other hand, was the Resurrection! The unexpectedness of God! This experience has surely encouraged the Church to never minimise the humanity of Christ, and, at the same time, encouraged his followers to never take themselves far too seriously!

Do we not see something of this, too, in the experience of Abraham, who had been promised descendants "as many as the sand on the shore of the sea" (Gen 22:17), and yet who was being asked by God to sacrifice his own son, Isaac – the only earthly means of achieving this promise? At a less dramatic level, it is a common experience.

The example of Judas, too, is relevant. He was Jesus' personal choice and his personal failure. He had been chosen and called; he had received the grace of apostolic ministry. Clearly he was an able man. He knew Jesus better than we do, but he did not understand him. He rejected his poverty, his weakness, his spirit. After the discourse of the Last Supper when Jesus said, "I no longer call you servants but friends" (Jn 15:15), it was Judas who was first addressed as "friend" by Jesus in the Garden of Gethsemane, and, in response, he betrayed him with that intimate sign of close friendship, a kiss!

It is a constant temptation within our thinking, within our communities, to want to try and straitjacket God. It is not possible to live in a Church that is like a double decker bus – the upstairs and the downstairs! People are often challenged by what might happen if they give unconditional assent to God's grace in their lives, if they allow the Holy Spirit to speak to them personally. One thing is for sure: not all the answers are written down.

In the end, it is only true love that can bear the deep suffering and disappointment of failure and which, at the same time, also remains open to hope. We see this once again in the Garden of the Tomb in the person of Mary Magdalene, the *Apostolorum Apostola*:

But Mary stood weeping outside the tomb, and as she wept she stooped to look into the tomb. And she saw two angels in white, sitting where the body of Jesus had lain, one at the head and one at the feet. They said to her, "Woman, why are you weeping?" She said to them, "They have taken away my Lord, and I do not know where they have laid him." Having said this, she turned around and saw Jesus standing, but she did not know that it was Jesus. Jesus said to her, "Woman, why are you weeping? Whom are you seeking?" Supposing him to be the gardener, she said to him, "Sir, if you have carried him away, tell me where you have laid him, and I will take him away." Jesus said to her, "Mary." She turned and said to him in Aramaic, "Rabboni!" (which means Teacher). Jesus said to her, "Do not cling to me, for I have not yet ascended to the Father; but go to my brothers and say to them, 'I am ascending to my Father and your Father, to my God and your God.'" Mary Magdalene went and announced to the disciples, "I have seen the Lord"—and that he had said these things to her. (Jn 20:11–18)

The other disciples, after looking inside the tomb, leave and go back home. Only Mary remains. Again, she looks into the tomb. Like the disciples on the road, she loved but doubted, saw but did not recognise. St Gregory says that "her love revealed him to her, and her doubt prevented her from knowing him." Nevertheless, she lingered; she looked again. "Thus it happened that she alone saw him," says St Gregory, "she who had remained behind to seek him, simply because a true good act involves the virtue of perseverance." By nature, we are God-seekers. How often things can be overlooked in haste. There remains in all of us, no matter how deformed we may be by sin, something of our original integrity before the fall, which triggers in us a desire for God who cannot be despatched or dismissed even by the senses. "For the lips of Truth have said, 'the one who perseveres to the end will be saved.'"

It is important to cultivate well the terrain in this garden of the tomb because it is a very real garden for priests and people. It lies between the shallow soil of disbelief and the rich soil where the seed grows best and where our flocks can most flourish by grace. The paralysing fear of failure or possible failure has no place in this pasture. What happened in this garden is not simply an episode in the life of Jesus and his followers. It is a revelation of what is possible for humanity by God's gift in understanding not 'what we are' but 'whose we are' and who God is!

"Woman, why are you weeping? Whom do you seek?" (Jn 20:15). Why indeed do we sometimes weep? Who is it whom we seek? This is similar to the question asked by Jesus to the first disciples at the beginning of John's Gospel (Jn 1:38) and which now, after the Resurrection, he changes from "what" to "whom". Our sufferings, our struggles speak also of our desires. There is great tenderness in Jesus' approach. He recognizes the tears. Indeed, he shed many of them himself. The second Mass for Forgiveness of Sins in the Roman Missal prays, "Almighty and most gentle God, who brought forth from the rock a fountain of living water for your thirsty people, so now bring forth from the hardness of our hearts tears of sorrow." Tears awaken the heart. How often people close down when faced with sufferings. The eyes that recognize suffering are located in the heart. How interesting, for example, are the verbs which are used in the parable of the Good Samaritan: 'he saw', 'had compassion', 'went to him', 'bound his wounds', 'poured oil and wine', 'sat him on his donkey', 'brought him to an inn', 'took care of him', 'gave money to the innkeeper', 'will repay whatever he owes'. They are a verbal, active description of the heart of Jesus – of his personal response to what he faced, what he saw. Indifference to the plight of others is like death. It is cold and lifeless.

Mary looked, and she looked a second time. There was nothing indifferent about this. In fact, her own distress, her suffering, and her doubting turned her round to face the one she thought of as the gardener, but who in fact was her Loved One.

Sister Ruth Burrows, an English Carmelite nun and spiritual writer, says that

> the human heart has to be broken open before it can receive God, and thus it was also with Jesus. And the deepest mystery of all is that we learn that

the Father's own heart is pierced. How can we enter into this pierced heart? Only by becoming like it, living in love at whatever the cost, paying the high price of loving. Too easily we assume that loving is a pleasurable experience. Most surely it is the only sweetness in life, but this must be understood correctly. . . . You simply cannot have love in this life without pain.

"Jesus said to her, 'Mary.' She turned and said to him in Aramaic, 'Rabboni!'" (Jn 20:16). She was looking for the dead, but it was the Living One who spoke to her. The barrier of death, of futility, and of failure was demolished at that moment. She seeking, but he revealing. Her pain dissolving in this wonderful and new grasp of reality beyond the grave. It has all the force and refreshment of a torrent of water that not only washes away the scales from our eyes, but through actually changing the landscape of our perceptions, plunges us into the great mystery of life, of God's love! Her perspective, her view, was immediately transformed.

In a letter written in April 1376 to Raimondo da Capua, in Avignon, St Catherine of Siena, who is clearly irritated with the pope's lack of decisiveness to return to Rome – partly because he thought that the cardinals were going to poison him! – wrote:

You see then that you must not complain or run away in time of darkness, because out of the darkness is born the light. . . . Because of impatience, patience is acquired, for people who are conscious of the vice of impatience become patient because of what they suffer. They are impatient with their impatience, more sad that they are sad at all than for anything else. And so, out of opposites we come to learn perfection without ever noticing it.

As Isaiah wrote at the time of the siege of Jerusalem: "When the Lord has given you the bread of suffering and the water of distress, he who is your teacher will hide no longer, and you will see your teacher with your own eyes. Whether you turn to right or left, you will hear these words behind you, 'This is the way, follow it!'" (Isa 30:20–21).

Father Robert Thomas, a French Trappist monk of the last century, used an illustration from his schooldays that helps us in a practical way. He noted that if you are drawing a line on a blackboard from one end to the other, looking all the while at the chalk as it travels, then the line you draw will inevitably become crooked. However, he noted, if you start to draw the same line looking not at the chalk but at the final point of destination – the ultimate point – then the line will be straight! Our eyes, not on ourselves, but on God!

When you pass from self to God, you change your center of gravity, you find your true center: God! "Made by God for himself," according to the famous saying of St Augustine, we do not find rest until we have found

God and repose in him. Otherwise, our heart is "unquiet", agitated instead of being tranquil. This moment of realisation, as it were, takes us outside ourselves, effaces us before God. And lo and behold, in losing ourselves to make room for him, we find ourselves in him. Everything in us then is well in place. Before it was dislocated – living in a realm of a reality without hope.

The Garden of the Tomb is the garden of our heart. That is where the battle and the victory is won: the hollow space that holds the great mystery of the womb, which is God's womb, hollowed out to give space for growth until the moment when, from the depths of darkness, a light is born and we see him as if for the first time. "From the womb before the dawn I begot you!" (Ps 110:3). This is where we find the Logos, the Risen Christ, the true Meaning of God!

The Garden of Paradise

My best friend is the one who brings out
the best in me.
Henry Ford

It is possible on occasion to feel that we have been driven from the Garden of Eden's peace and tranquillity, or even left at the foot of the mountain of Tabor, or outside the gate of Gethsemane, or locked up in a room while the victory of Christ is discovered, or just left in a garden with little possibility of keeping the weeds at bay, but there is a purpose in all of this, too. As St Paul says, "We know that for those who love God all things work together for good, for those who are called according to his purpose!" (Rm 8:28).

We come now to the Garden of Paradise. We make this visit, of course, from afar – indeed, from a great distance! Returning to the Letter to the Hebrews we share the conviction that "here we have no lasting city, but we are looking for the city that is to come" (Heb

13:14). We cannot completely describe this city, this paradise, but we are given many clues from personal experiences, including those of Saints Peter, Paul, and John.

St Peter in his second letter takes us back to the moment of the Transfiguration:

> It was not any cleverly invented myths that we were repeating when we brought you the knowledge of the power and the coming of our Lord Jesus Christ; we had seen his majesty for ourselves. He was honoured and glorified by God the Father, when the Sublime Glory itself spoke to him and said, 'This is my Son, the Beloved; he enjoys my favour.' We heard this ourselves, spoken from heaven, when we were with him on the holy mountain. So we have confirmation of what was said in prophecies; and you will be right to depend on prophecy and take it as a lamp for lighting a way through the dark until the dawn comes and the morning star rises in your minds. (2 Pt 1:16–19)

Evidently, the experience of the Transfiguration made a very deep impression upon St Peter. St Paul, too, relates a profoundly personal experience in his second letter to the church at Corinth, and he struggles to express it precisely:

I will move on to the visions and revelations I have had from the Lord. I know a man in Christ who, fourteen years ago, was caught up – whether still in the body or out of the body, I do not know; God knows – right into the third heaven. I do know, however, that this same person – whether in the body or out of the body, I do not know; God knows – was caught up into paradise and heard things which must not and cannot be put into human language. I will boast about a man like that, but not about anything of my own except my weaknesses. If I should decide to boast, I should not be made to look foolish, because I should only be speaking the truth; but I am not going to, in case anyone should begin to think I am better than he can actually see and hear me to be. (2 Cor 12:1–6)

Then, St John shares with us that cosmic vision of heaven as something which is completely new but where a wonderful intimacy with God exists:

Then I saw a new heaven and a new earth, for the first heaven and the first earth had passed away, and the sea was no more. And I saw the holy city, the new Jerusalem, coming down out of heaven from God, prepared as a bride adorned for her husband. And I heard a loud voice from the throne saying, "Behold, the dwelling place of God is with man. He will dwell with them, and they will be his people, and God himself will be with them as their God. He will wipe away every tear from their eyes, and death shall be no more, neither shall there be mourning, nor crying, nor pain anymore, for the former things have passed away." And he who was seated on the throne said, "Behold, I am making all things new." (Rv 21:1–5)

In Dante's epic poem, in the thirty-third canto of the *Paradiso*, he tells us that when St Bernard of Clairvaux introduces him to the vision of God, "from this point on my capacity to see was greater than words can show, which fail in the face of such seeing." He subsequently says something which is quite stunning and links so well with our thoughts on the gardening that has taken place in the kingdom throughout the ages. He writes as he gazes into the divine light, perceiving a connection with everything throughout creation finding its unity in this illumination, that "in its depths I saw gathered, bound with love in one volume, what is scattered in gatherings through the universe!" This speaks of a gathering whose effects are beyond imagination, as it were of all the virtuous redeemed fruits of the universe collected into this point and place. Hugh of St Victor says that the whole of the universe is like a book written by God's finger!

Returning to St Paul in his second letter to the church at Corinth, he writes:

We know that when the tent that we live in on earth is folded up, there is a house built by God for us, an everlasting home not made by human hands, in the heavens. In this present state, it is true, we groan as we wait with longing to put on our heavenly home over the other; we should like to be found wearing clothes and not without them. Yes, we groan and find it a burden being still in this tent, not that we want to strip it off, but to put the second garment over it and to have what must die taken up into life. This is the purpose for which God made us, and he has given us the pledge of the Spirit. (2 Cor 5:1–5)

The hidden wisdom of God found in the Scriptures helps us grasp the existential element of this 'here and now'. The parable of the Labourers in the Vineyard from Matthew, for example, is well known:

"For the kingdom of heaven is like a master of a house who went out early in the morning to hire labourers for his vineyard. After agreeing with the labourers for a denarius a day, he sent them into his vineyard. And going out about the third hour he saw others standing idle in the marketplace, and to them he said, 'You go into the vineyard too, and whatever is right I will give you.' So they went. Going out again about the sixth hour and the ninth hour, he did the same. And about the eleventh hour he went out and found others standing. And he said to them, 'Why do you stand here idle all day?' They said to him, 'Because no one has hired us.' He said to them, 'You go into the vineyard too.' And when evening came, the owner of the vineyard said to his foreman, 'Call the labourers and pay them their wages, beginning with the last, up to the first.' And when those hired about the eleventh hour came, each of them received a denarius. Now when those hired first came, they thought they would receive more, but each of them also received a denarius. And on receiving it they grumbled at the master of the house, saying, 'These last worked only one hour, and you have made them equal to us who have borne the burden of the day and the scorching heat.' But he replied to one of them, 'Friend, I am doing you no wrong. Did you not agree with me for a denarius? Take what belongs to you and go. I choose to give to this last worker as I give to you. Am I not allowed to do what I choose with what belongs to me? Or do you begrudge my generosity?' So the last will be first, and the first last." (Mt 20:1–16)

The moment of truth came at the end of the day, as it will at the end of all days! The wage that was received by those who came last bore no relation to the work they had undertaken at the eleventh hour. The system of merit and reward was overthrown. In the kingdom of God, Jesus gives all for nothing. It must have been as shocking then as it remains difficult today to accept, even to understand, as we ponder this reality of gratuitous mercy. God pays the cost of our idleness – he pays the cost of our idolatry.

But what does this mean for us who are the cultivators of the Lord's vineyard? After all, we share with Christ the responsibility for the kingdom here on earth which ultimately has consequences in heaven, too, as we read in the Gospels (see Mt 19:28; Lk 22:28–30).

Adam was put into Eden by God to cultivate it, but his neglect of his tenure – his eye turned solely towards his own gain – brought about his eviction from paradise. No, our eyes, our efforts are to be elsewhere when we begin to cultivate the garden of our soul as well as the vineyard of the Lord, the field which is his Church. It is a well-cultivated life that brings forth the fruit that is Christ. It works towards the burgeoning of that fruit which is for the kingdom rather than towards its own enrichment. Revisiting Gabriel Marcel's image, a perfectly ripe apple is only one stage away from rotting! We must maintain a sense of humour, of proportion. As Pope Francis said to newly ordained bishops who were beginning their episcopal ministry, as well as to the people of Tacloban: "God was there before you were!"

St John Chrysostom says that the various times allotted for the workers – the early morning, the third, sixth, ninth, and eleventh hours – refer to our personal situations here and now, the various stages of our life, and that the produce of the vineyard are the virtues cultivated through the commandments of the Lord. The Lord gives us many opportunities to come to him throughout our entire lives, indeed at every moment. What we do with these depends upon what we are looking for or looking at!

We notice in the parable that the first group, the one which became last of all, was the one that negotiated its own terms of reward, whereas the other groups were 'called'. They did not negotiate their own deal: "The last will be first, and the first last."

St Gregory the Great in his commentary on this Gospel says:

> The sheepfold of our holy Church receives goats together with lambs, but as the gospel bears witness when the judge comes he will separate the good from the evil as a shepherd sets the sheep apart from the goats [Mt 25:32]. Those who are subject to the pleasures of their bodies here cannot be counted in the sheepfold there. The judge will separate from the ranks of the humble those who now exalt themselves on the horns of pride. Those who share the heavenly faith in this life, but seek the earth with their whole desire, cannot obtain the kingdom of heaven.

How often have we heard the saying "beauty is in the eye of the beholder"? What Jesus says, moreover, is,

> "The eye is the lamp of the body. So, if your eye is healthy, your whole body will be full of light, but if your eye is bad, your whole body will be full of

darkness. If then the light in you is darkness, how great is the darkness!" (Mt 6:22–23)

This text was a continuation of the Lord's teaching about prayer in Matthew which we considered at the outset. We journey from the heart, the inner storeroom, to the whole body. It is the eye that directs the heart to a goal on earth or in heaven.

The idea of light, of course, is symbolic in that it represents the great longings of human life. We can sometimes find ourselves in the dumps, in the darkness, but the desire for light, deep within us, within our souls, indicates to us that darkness is not its natural and final state. We are made for something more. Even in the darkest hour there is something to be hoped for. God made us for greatness, to be radiant. Father Alfred Delp, a Jesuit who was put to death by the Nazis in 1945, said: "We are never more soul sick than when we become confused and find ourselves helpless to cope with a situation. That is the primary meaning of the prayer 'Send Your Radiant Light'".

A story is recorded of a conversation between St Francis of Assisi and Brother Leo. Francis said to Leo, "Do you know, brother, what purity of heart is?" Leo replied, "It's not having any fault with which to reproach yourself." "Then", said Francis, "I understand your sadness, Leo, because one always has something about which to reproach himself." "Yes," said Leo, "which is precisely what makes me despair at arriving one day at purity of heart." "O Brother Leo, believe me," said Francis, "don't worry so much about the purity of your soul. Turn your gaze toward God. Admire him. Rejoice in what he is, he, all holiness. Thank him because of himself. Having a pure heart is exactly that, little brother. And when you are thus turned towards God, above all do not turn back to yourself at all. Don't ask where you stand with God. The sadness of not being perfect and finding yourself a sinner is still a human sentiment – too human! You must lift your gaze higher, much higher. There is God, the immensity of God and his unalterable splendour. The pure heart is the one that does not cease adoring the living and true Lord. . . . It is enough for it that God should be God. In that alone it finds all its peace, all its pleasure. And God himself is therefore all its holiness. . . . Our nothingness, you see, if it is accepted, becomes the free space where God is still able to create. The Lord does not allow his glory to be carried off by anyone. . . . But, 'he takes the poor man [by the hand], and pulls him out of the mud, and makes him sit with the princes of his people' (Ps 113:7b–8), so that he may see his glory. God then becomes the jewel of his soul. To contemplate the glory of God, to discover that God is God, eternally God, beyond what we are or can be, to rejoice fully in what he is, to be in ecstasy before his eternal youth and to thank him for himself, for his unfailing mercy, that is the most profound demand of that love which the Spirit of the Lord does not cease to pour into our hearts. That's what it is to have a pure heart . . . [to]

keep nothing of yourself. Sweep out everything, even that sharp perception of your own distress. . . . Have nothing more than the glory of God, become irradiated by it. God is, that is enough!"

We return to our original question: not 'what am I?' but 'whose am I?' Our poor mortal frames are often dazzled by the light of God or by the attraction of something entirely different, so this rhetorical question is important to remember.

I came across a text which also serves as a useful illustration. Susan Griffin, in her book *Pornography and Silence: Culture's Revenge Against Nature*, says of those who are hooked on pornography that the voyeur sees but does not sense. "He is not touched by reality. And yet, in his mind, he can believe he possesses reality. For he has control over these images which he makes and he shapes them to his own will." Ultimately, eyes upon himself, he creates a different world. He has become 'ipsatory'.

Yet, we are encouraged in the Psalm, "My eyes are always on the Lord, for he rescues my feet from the snare" – out of the snare (Ps 25:15).

"It is the only thing we can do", said Etty Hillesum. "I see no alternative, each of us ought to destroy in himself all that he thinks he ought to destroy in others."

There is a rabbinic tradition that says that when the Messiah comes he will sit at the city gates as a beggar, and most will look upon him as an ugly sight. "He grew up before him like a young plant, and like a root out of dry ground; he had no form or majesty that we should look at him, and no beauty that we should desire him" (Is 53:2).

St Teresa of Calcutta, who was used to seeing Christ in what appeared humanly ugly, knew the importance of seeing beyond the disagreeable. When she wrote to the Missionaries of Charity on the Solemnity of the Annunciation in 1993, she talked of the importance of seeing Christ with the eyes of the soul: "Until you know deep inside that Jesus thirsts for you, you cannot begin to know who He wants to be for you. Or who He wants you to be for Him."

This seeing is an understanding born not of learning but of wisdom. It is something that enters the bloodstream and changes our vision.

Pope St John Paul II wrote in his autobiographical reflection that "the Minister of the Word must possess and pass on that knowledge of God which is not a mere deposit of doctrinal truths but a personal and living experience of the Mystery." It reminds us of what Pope St Paul VI wrote of in *Evangelii Nuntiandi* when he noted that the most effective and authentic teachers are those whose personal lives give testimony to what they teach.

Blessed Guerric of Igny, a Cistercian abbot of the twelfth century, in one of his sermons which considers the implication of Christ's entrance into Jerusalem on a donkey, writes:

> I hear mankind say to the Creator, "I will not serve."
> "Then, I will serve you," his Creator says to man.

"You sit down, I will minister, I will wash your feet.
You rest; I will bear your weariness, your infirmities.
Use me as you like in all you need, not only as your
slave but also as your beast of burden and as your
own property. If you are tired or burdened I will
carry both you and your burden, so that I may be
the first to keep my own law: 'Bear one another's
burdens' we read, 'and so you will fulfil the law of
Christ' [Gal 6:2]. If you are hungry or thirsty . . . I
am ready to be slaughtered that 'you may eat my
flesh and drink my blood' [Jn 6:53–57]. . . . If you
are led into captivity or sold, here I am, sell me and
redeem yourself at my cost. . . . If you are ill and
afraid to die I will die for you."

God has created us for greatness! He has created
us for paradise. We pray that throughout our lives, in
whatever garden we find ourselves, we may have always
the grace to expand to the greatness of the size of Christ,
rather than shrink to the size of self.

"But we impart a secret and hidden wisdom of
God," says St Paul to the church in Corinth, "which
God decreed before the ages for our glory. None of the
rulers of this age understood this, for if they had, they
would not have crucified the Lord of glory. But, as it
is written, 'What no eye has seen, nor ear heard, nor
the heart of man imagined, what God has prepared for
those who love him' – these things God has revealed to

us through the Spirit. For the Spirit searches everything, even the depths of God" (1 Cor 2:7–10).

The Imaginary Garden

Why, sometimes I've believed as many as
six impossible things before breakfast.
Lewis Carroll

The vision we have for the garden of our soul will determine the seeds we allow to be planted there, which will make it either a true or an unreal, imaginary garden. What and where we plant, and what or not we nurture when planted, has consequences. In the parable of the sower, seed was spread over four different soils, only one of which allowed it to germinate. Some may consider it careless of the sower to be so profligate. Seed was expensive, and a good harvest guaranteed a welcome income. The sower was hoping, however, that no matter what obstacle faced the seed, the soil would change and become the humus that would foster it and give it the growth that would eventually mature into fruit. Maturity, more often than not, is achieved through struggle rather than by a carefree life.

The ground on which we stand not only has to be well prepared but also truthful, humble ground, firm enough to withstand falsity and fraudulency. The nurturing of it needs prudent discernment. When St Paul speaks of the discernment of spirits in the First Letter to the Corinthians, he uses an interesting turn of phrase, *diakriseis pneumatōn* (1 Cor 12:10), which is an apt image of sifting coins. Anyone who has had to count the Sunday collection knows how important this sifting is. Unlike the widow's mite, the putting of tokens and foreign change into the collection adds nothing to charitable works or to the payment of bills.

The creation of an illusory world is a consequence of a lack of groundedness. As Alice in Wonderland puts it, "If I had a world of my own, everything would be nonsense. Nothing would be what it is, because everything would be what it isn't. And contrary wise, what is, it wouldn't be. And what it wouldn't be, it would. You see?"

Humility as a virtue has had a bad press over the last two centuries partly due to it being forced into a form that was actually its opposite. Its extremes lie between sycophancy and humiliation. Dickens portrays the epitome of the first in *David Copperfield*'s character Uriah Heep: "'When I was quite a young boy,' said Uriah, 'I got to know what umbleness did, and I took to it. I ate umble pie with an appetite. . . . "People like to be above you" says father, "keep yourself down." I am very umble to the present moment, Master Copperfield, but I've got a little power!'" Uriah used obsequiousness for personal advantage over others and it worked within a vain and un-egalitarian society. He used the inverse of societal mores which were just as unreal and silly. Then, at the other end of the scale, there's the aggressive knockdown and self-righteous shaming and humiliation of people, the cruel and hypocritical boast when someone makes a slip in life. Cancel culture, for example, unlike excommunication, is unforgiving. Excommunication, when issued, acts as a warning, a shot across the bows.

These extremes, and all shades in between, are forgeries of healthy life and living. Personal virtue will always reflect what lies deep within the soul – the sweet perfume of grace or the iron filings of bitterness, resentment, and pride. "For figs are not gathered from thorn bushes, nor are grapes picked from a bramble bush" (Lk 6:44). Jesus speaks like an experienced gardener when he warns those prone to self-deceit that "either make the tree good and its fruit good, or make the tree bad and its fruit bad, for the tree is known by its fruit" (Mt 12:33).

Staying close to reality and developing a self-understanding that leads to human flourishing is found in the Beatitudes, where we discover the heart of Jesus' spirituality (Mt 5:3–12, Lk 6:20–23). There, we find preserved the asceticism that is in Jesus' wisdom for living, his values for life. They are like little codes that open up for us an unexpected way to freedom. On the face of it they seem to stand for things which are the very opposite of how we look upon blessedness. But the Greek *makarios* means 'blessed': beatitude is another way of saying blessedness. The Beatitudes imply that the way we deal with life or reality is the key to this blessedness. Romano Guardini observed that "in the Beatitudes something of the celestial grandeur breaks through. They are no mere formulas for superior ethics, but tidings of sacred and supreme reality's entry into the world." Like stepping-stones, they offer us a path through life, which has been trod by countless others. They are signposts of wisdom, deeply rooted in what it is to be most truly human, to be grounded in God and to reflect the face of Christ in our own humanity. This re-evaluation of values as presented by Jesus points to humble pathways that lead to "the freedom of the glory of the children of God" of which St Paul speaks (Rm 8:21). As St Irenaeus puts it, "The glory of God is man fully alive!"

While humility is not listed among the seven theological and cardinal virtues in the *Catechism*, it is, nonetheless, the ground on which all virtue stands or falls. The classical Roman conception of virtue as strength of human character (a characteristic not shared in Judeo-Christian thought) was redefined by St Augustine as that which most contributes to human flourishing (*beatitudo*) – the blessedness that finds its ultimate goal in the enjoyment of God. For Augustine, humility was simply the grace of Christ that characterises and most underpins the Christian life. It is, as it were, the groundedness of grace, for, as Aquinas said, "grace perfects nature".

St Anthony of the Desert thought of humility as the means for navigating through the snares of evil, preventing us from deviating from our true course. Observing that those who live turbulent lives do not always see reality as it is, he uses the image of gazing into a bowl of newly scooped water from a murky stream which prevents a clear reflection. Once the turbulence has subsided and the sediment has settled through stillness, however, we begin to see ourselves more clearly in the reflection as well as our sins in the dregs lying at the bottom of the bowl.

St Athanasius says that "he [the Word of God] became man so that we might become God." Like the Beatitudes, we might think this is an odd way of expressing our divine prospects, but in the earthly reality of our existence our longing is found in rising higher rather than sinking lower – to expand to the size of Christ rather than sink to the size of self. That reality is closer to the earth that, nevertheless, still awaits the breath of the Spirit.

St Catherine of Siena, who was never one to be reticent in advising clergy, including the pope, wrote to a priest, "Self-knowledge is the dwelling in which we discover our own lowliness, and this makes us humble. There we find the knowledge of God's goodness, too, and in this light a warmth, a fire of love, is born in us – so gently that all bitterness becomes sweet, everything weak grows strong, and all the ice of selfish love melts away."

The intent of her message was clear but, as in all her letters, it was not lacking in encouragement.

St Paul, in his Letter to the Philippians (Phil 2:6–8), was anxious to press not only the point of Christ's humility but also of a loving obedience that springs from it. This speaks of a radical openness grounded in humility, for sure, but coming from a heart shaped by an unimaginable depth of love for God and the human race.

Without the substructure of humility, the ascetical life will be an impossible mountain to climb. Hebrews puts it this way:

> You need milk, not solid food, for everyone who lives on milk is unskilled in the word of righteousness, since he is a child. But solid food is for the mature, for those who have their powers of discernment trained by constant practice to distinguish good from evil." (Heb 5:12–14)

The word of righteousness is, of course, developed from a humble attentiveness to God's Word. There we begin to listen to our heart and to hear the echo of God's Word reverberating within. It expands the heart, teaching us to be vigilant and to listen at a deep level to reality. It is a process of refinement which, in the presence of God, enables us to become more sensitive and less prone to harmful blustering. The Holy Spirit within the soul forms a respectful sensitivity not only to God but also towards others. How clearly we see this in Jesus' submissiveness to his parents on returning to Nazareth after his disappearance in Jerusalem. There is a telling phrase at the end of that account which summarises the hidden greatness of that moment: "and his mother treasured all these things in her heart" (Lk 2:51). In so many ways, this too is fundamental to our life of obedience as priests – *ob audire*, which translates the Greek *hypakoē* – to hear or look 'below or behind' the word. In other words, our *'submission* to what is *heard'* is our response to the voice of the Lord. "For if anyone is a hearer of the word and not a doer, he is like a man who looks intently at his natural face in a mirror. For he looks at himself and goes away and at once forgets what he was like" (Jm 1:23–24). Pope Francis speaks of this as spiritual Alzheimer's which "consists in losing the memory of our personal 'salvation history', our past history with the Lord and our 'first love' (Rv 2:4). It involves a progressive decline in the spiritual faculties which in the long or short run greatly handicaps a person by making him incapable of doing anything on his own, living in a state of absolute dependence on his often imaginary perceptions. We see it . . . in those who build walls and routines around themselves, and thus become more and more the slaves of idols carved by their own hands."

This touches upon two important poles in our lives: prayer, the privileged place where we discern the movement of the Spirit; and action, where what deeply reverberates within us leads us to live it out – to act with an ear that is always open to the Holy Spirit.

The *examen conscientiae* that St Ignatius developed in his teachings should really be translated as the examination of our *consciousness*. How conscious are we of the action of the Holy Spirit, more than of our sinful traits? C.S. Lewis once noted that a humble man "will not be thinking about humility: he will not be thinking about himself at all." William of St-Thierry describes St Bernard as someone who seemed to bring the anointing of the Holy Spirit to everything he did throughout the day. Our ministry is outward looking. We, too, are called to spread this same unction in all that we do. As Pope Francis has often alluded, the anointing that we receive as priests is not for ourselves but for those whom our ministry touches in our priestly service. The wisdom of John Cassian encourages us to keep all the recesses of our heart "under constant surveillance" and says that "the traces of whatever arises there must be prudently considered. This is in case some mental beast – lion or dragon – might, in passing through, leave there its harmful traces."

This line of thought raises for me a question as to the use of blogs, etc. by the warring clergy. I have long lost interest in what is said on them, but what they often express and profess to espouse, frequently forsaking charity, is surely discerned from a very different spirit that is deeply harmful and highly scandalous. Marcus Aurelius' dictum that 'more grievous are the consequences of anger than the causes of it' stands good. The tyranny of superiority is something to which St Paul alludes in his first letter to the church in Thessalonica:

> Nor did we seek glory from people, whether from you or from others, though we could have made demands as apostles of Christ. But we were gentle among you, like a nursing mother taking care of her own children. So, being affectionately desirous of you, we were ready to share with you not only the gospel of God but also our own selves, because you had become very dear to us. (1 Th 2:6–8)

While the internet has much to offer us, an undisciplined and uncritical use of it not infrequently leads to misinformation and fake news that leads people away from what is true as well as prudent. When it is used to persuade people to one's own opinion, it becomes a serious matter. Pope St Clement I offers us a salutary observation: "For Christ belongs to those who are humble-minded, not to those who vaunt themselves over the flock. The sceptre of God's majesty, the Lord Jesus Christ, did not come with an ostentatious show of arrogance or haughtiness – even though he could have done so – but with a humble mind, just as the Holy Spirit spoke concerning him." It is the mustard seed alone that grows into the most impressive plant in the garden and one that gives shelter to others (Mt 13:32). In one of his sermons, St Augustine speaks of the pride that changed angels into devils and of the humility that makes men equal to angels. We find a salutary caution in the book of Revelation for the one who "accuses the brethren" day and night but who, in the end, will be the one who is thrown down (Rv 12:9–10).

It is good to recall how God views us, "for the Lord sees not as man sees: man looks on the outward appearance, but the Lord looks on the heart" (1 Sm 16:7). When Moses was being harshly criticised by his own sister and brother, God shocks them by saying, in contrast, that he considers Moses to be "the most humble of men, the humblest man on earth. . . . He is at home in my house; I speak with him mouth to mouth, plainly and not in riddles, and he sees the form of the Lord" (Nb 12:3, 7b–8). For good reason St Cyril of Alexandria declares, "We must be distinguished not by our clothing, but by what we really are." Or as John Buchan put it, "A fool tries to look different: a clever man looks the same and is different." This would merit a chapter on its own.

The seed of God's Word is the Father's gift, and when allowed to flourish it bears fruit that reflects the image of his own Son within us (Gal 4:6–7). Returning to St James' letter,

> Do not be deceived, my beloved brothers. Every good gift and every perfect gift is from above, coming down from the Father of lights, with whom there is no variation or shadow due to change. Of his own will he brought us forth by the word of truth, that

we should be a kind of firstfruits of his creatures.
Know this, my beloved brothers: let every person be
quick to hear, slow to speak, slow to anger; for the
anger of man does not produce the righteousness of
God. Therefore put away all filthiness and rampant
wickedness and receive with meekness the implanted
word, which is able to save your souls. But be doers of
the word, and not hearers only, deceiving yourselves.
(Jm 1:16–22)

This seed begins to bolster us against the sins that corrupt
and destroy. St John says, "No one born of God makes
a practice of sinning, for God's seed abides in him; and
he cannot keep on sinning, because he has been born of
God" (1 Jn 3:9). James later describes a humble person
as someone who gives first place to God in his life and,
conscious of his weakness and disobedience to his calling as a Christian, speaks no evil of others or boasts of
himself (Jm 4:7–17). As Hermas wrote, "Watch out for
the double soul for it is an evil and senseless thing, and
it uproots many from the faith, even those who are very
firm and faithful. For this double soul is the daughter of
the devil and does great harm, to the servants of God."

There is a remarkable passage from Blessed Guerric
of Igny's sermon on the Feast of the Epiphany. He pitches
his text between the birth of the Saviour at Christmas
and our birth in the waters of Baptism: "That which we
celebrated up to today is the birth of Christ, that which
we celebrate today is our own birth." He uses the cure

of Naaman the Leper as an illustration from the Old Testament (2 Kgs 5) that prefigures our Baptism and its continual renewal through the exercise of humility. He addresses the leper:

> Listen at least, Naaman, to your servants, your humble friends, your trusty counsellors. Naaman was going back, indignant at the man of God whom he had consulted. But they said, "Father, if the prophet had bidden you to do some great thing you certainly would have done it." Trustworthy advice indeed, full of reason and wisdom, as are the suggestions of man's rational feelings, which God has reserved for himself as witness against man himself. . . . But Elisha expressed himself unambiguously, "Wash seven times and you will be cleansed." For he was aware that Christ's humility, which we must imitate if we wish to be perfectly cleansed, is sevenfold in its virtue. Its first virtue is that although he was rich he became poor; its second, that he carried poverty to its extreme limit and was laid in a manger; its third, that he was subject to his mother; its fourth, that today he bent his head beneath a servant's hands; its fifth, that he so bore with a disciple who was a thief and a traitor; its sixth, that he was so meek before an unjust judge; its seventh, that he was so forgiving in interceding with his Father for those who crucified him. You follow in the giant's footsteps in these things, even if from afar, if you love poverty,

if you love its extreme limit among the poor, if you are subject to the monastery's discipline, if you allow one less than yourself to command you, if you bear patiently with false brethren, if you overcome with meekness when you are judged, if you requite with charity those who make you unjustly suffer. This humility truly rebaptises us with no infringement of the sole baptism, for it does not repeat Christ's death but renews the mortification and burial of sins and carries out in very truth what is represented in outward form by that baptism. . . . Hence Scripture does well to say of Naaman that his flesh was restored like the flesh of a little child.

In the Bible, the leitmotif of humility is found throughout, often unnoticed, as is fitting for such a modest grace that supports all other characteristics of goodness and mercy. Charles de Foucauld, in his retreat notes in Nazareth, saw this very clearly:

My God, you have always taught humility by word and example that you have made it one of your chief characteristics. You who were so great, teach me, who am so small and mean, to be humble like you. Your humility was to be an example for all. You so comprehended the difference between the Creator and his creatures that you wished your human nature (though it made up one Person with your divine nature) to render the homage of an infinite humility to the Divinity, whose infinite grandeur you were able clearly to comprehend. So, if you choose to be humble, how much more should I be humble; I, for whom St Augustine said, "humility is the truth," should look upon myself as nothing, as a worm. Worse in some respects than the fallen spirits, not in all respects, but in that of having abused your grace and in having sinned innumerable times after having received your pardon.

The creation of an unreal, imaginary garden established upon poor soil eventually begins to poison the things we plant there. All the other gardens we have considered are built on reality, and those gardens alone possess the potential for a true and abundant harvest, both in the life of the individual and in the life of the Church.

The Enclosed Garden

*Once in our world, a stable had something in it
that was bigger than our whole world.*

C.S. Lewis

We have journeyed in these reflections from the garden of earthly paradise through to the garden of Joseph of Arimathea where Jesus appeared to Mary Magdalene as a gardener, an *hortulanus*, and finally to the garden of the heavenly paradise.

There remains, however, one other important garden to consider, whose beauty is so delicate and refined that it is hidden from the eye – the *Hortus Conclusus*, or the Enclosed Garden, a lesser-known name given by tradition to Mary, the Virgin Mother of Jesus.

This garden is first mentioned in the Song of Songs of King Solomon: "A garden locked is my sister, my bride, a spring locked, a fountain sealed" (Sg 4:12). It is an important text. The Jews sing from these dramatic and passionate poems during their Passover celebrations, while Christians use them as an illustration of the love of Christ for his Church. The imagery is often called upon in patristic writings and in liturgical texts in direct reference to Mary: "You are an enclosed garden, O Mother of God, an enclosed garden, a fountain sealed: arise, my love!" It speaks of Mary's virginity, which is not simply a physical reality but a spiritual one too.

In the view of the medieval and Renaissance ages, the enclosed garden, more than any other, speaks of the hidden life, the place where the Holy Spirit is actively at work. The *hortus conclusus* as portrayed in the literature and paintings of the period is a place protected by a high wall; an area safe from public intrusion, capturing the beauty of nature within its confines, keeping at bay foraging animals and invasive plants; and a place, importantly, where medicinal herbs can be grown.

There is a long and interesting history to the development of the enclosed garden from its origin in Mesopotamia to the Roman Empire, but the monastic garden, above all, preserved the ancient tradition with its central tree or fountain and its quadrants divided by paths branching off from the centre to form a cross – the *arbor et fons vitae*! The cloister, thus divided, with the primordial tree at the centre, was a layout of Eden symbolising the rivers of paradise and the blood flowing from the wounds in Christ's hands and feet. This cloister was divided into equal parts, corresponding to the four corners of the created world.

The medieval period often painted the scene of the Annunciation taking place in such an *hortus conclusus* (e.g., Fra Angelico and Leonardo da Vinci). It is not easy to know what historic foundation this was thought to have, but it certainly resonates with the theological and mystical interpretation of the Song of Songs and of the books of Genesis and Revelation. Wherever the Annunciation took place, one thing is for sure: that on that tiny piece of ground, an event of immense importance happened which was the start of the greatest love story the world has ever known. It makes the sublime poems of Solomon a fitting description of the depth of that mystery which incorporated God's love for the entire human race:

> O my dove, in the clefts of the rock,
> in the crannies of the cliff,
> let me see your face,
> let me hear your voice,
> for your voice is sweet,
> and your face is lovely. (Sg 2:14)

St Bernard of Clairvaux was one of the most extensive commentators on this book and interprets this great canticle in reference to the tender love between God and the soul. God, who is deeply in love with the soul, desires the soul's love in return. This is the most intimate love possible and is so touchingly expressed in the analogy of the love of a young girl and her shepherd boy. By a further analogy, St Bernard observes that this ardour is a foreshadowing of the love of God for Mary and, through that same analogy, offers us an awareness of God's love for his Bride, the Church. The Song of Songs portrays something which is both deeply private and intimate and yet which of its nature flows out into a wider context. That Catholic "both/and" is part of the genius of St Bernard's commentary. The enclosed garden where this meeting takes place is the chamber of God's hidden purpose not only for the soul but for the life of the whole world.

St Bernard uses multiple sermons on this book of the Bible to make known the depth of love in a mystery which is being revealed to the world through the Incarnation and in our redemption. He calls this the *magnum pietatis sacramentum* – the great mystery of godliness! Not an idea, but a person who wishes to make all people one with the Father and with himself – "that they may be one even as we are one, I in them and you in me, that they may become perfectly one" (Jn 17:22–23). This is the mystical union of Christ with his Church, and speaking of this St Bernard says: "Truly I must love Him perfectly, in whom I have my being, my life and my knowledge. . . . Clearly, Lord Jesus, that man is worthy of death who refuses to live for you: indeed, he is already dead. And he who does not know you by love knows nothing. And he who cares to be for anything else but you, is destined for nothingness, and is become nothing."

The epic drama in the Song of Songs tells the story of a country girl from the village of Shulam who, because of her great beauty, attracts the attention of the king. She is content as she is and would rather stay with her shepherd boy, but her brothers, who are ambitious, are aware of the advantages that a relationship with the king would bring to their family, and so she is brought to the harem, the most intimate dwelling in the royal palace. Here, her companions do their utmost to distract the king to choose one of them to be his bride, but the king is not distracted: "As a lily among brambles, so is my love among the young women!" (Sg 2:2). The Shulamite girl is mocked by the fair-complexioned girls for the darkness of her skin, which is a result of her work in the vineyard under the sun's intense heat (Sg 1:6). Exposure to the sun was avoided by wealthier people. They sarcastically refer to her as the "fairest among women" (Sg 1:8). Indeed, she admits wittily, "I am very dark, but beautiful, O daughters of Jerusalem" (Sg 1:5). The king tries everything to win her love, and although he sings her praises, the girl's heart goes out to the shepherd boy who is so alive to her in spite of his absence. The king allows her to return home. Her brothers, whom she describes as little foxes, make it difficult for her to meet the boy, but she imagines him looking for her with the youth and delicacy of a bounding gazelle: "The voice of my beloved! Behold he comes, leaping over the mountains, bounding over the hills" (Sg 2:8), she gasps. He appears, looking through the lattice, and beckons her, "Arise, my love, my beautiful one, and come away; for behold, the winter is past, the rain is over and gone. The flowers appear on the earth, the time of singing has come and the cooing of the turtle-dove is heard once more in our land" (Sg 2:10–12). Her longing for him, although they are separated, is so great that she cries: "I sought him whom my soul loves" (Sg 3:1). Finally, she finds him, holds him close, and will not let him go until he agrees to return home with her. The king, however, turns up at this point in the hope of a betrothal. He takes her away, but the shepherd follows and pleads with her instead to be his bride. She is profoundly stirred by the extent and depth of his love. Her companions begin to realise that there is something remarkable about this affair, and even though the king pleads with her not to depart, he finally has to let her go. She meets her lover and promises her complete love to him as they return to the apple tree in the garden. So ends the story – but what a story! Such fervour, such a longing desire for each other is an affirmation that there is no power greater, no force more terrible than love: "for love is strong as death" (Sg 8:6). Love is unconquerable!

The love of God is something that compels, certainly, but it has to be received and returned freely. How wonderful, therefore, that this image is so readily thought of as an image of Mary, who in her virginity was to give birth to her son and who was ever to remain also a virgin. This passionate love is the backdrop against which we see the glory of Mary and the restless love of the Church for Christ.

Behold, you are beautiful, my love,
behold, you are beautiful!
Your eyes are doves
behind your veil. . . .
Your lips are like a scarlet thread,
and your mouth is lovely. (Sg 4:1, 3)

Just as the Church uses the Song of Songs during
Advent as an image to describe her own longing for
Christ, so it also expresses the lowly maiden of Nazareth's
deep longing for God – all that is within her yearning
for the Lord, her Shepherd Boy, her King. Like the
Shulamite, the girl of Nazareth was not prompted in
any way by the gain of preferment, but by a deep love
whose fulfilment comes with giving, and losing oneself
in the giving, as the priceless pearl bought by selling all
else (Mt 13:46). The quest for wisdom is the quest for
the beloved.

You have captivated my heart, my sister, my bride;
you have captivated my heart with one glance
        of your eyes,
with one jewel of your necklace.
How beautiful is your love, my sister, my bride!
How much better is your love than wine,
and the fragrance of your oils than any spice!
(Sg 4:9–10)

Our Lady stands as a sign of the reality and beauty and intimacy of the interior life. "Who is this who looks down like the dawn, beautiful as the moon, bright as the sun, awesome as an army with banners?" (Sg 6:10). She is the archetype of what the Church should be in all its perfection and as such holds a revered place within all the gardens of our dioceses and parishes as well as our own lives. She was the first to embody this profound relationship of the divine with humanity, not simply in conceiving the Lord with such willing hospitality, which says much about her character. She made room in her thoughts for God's thoughts – in her heart for God's heart. She made room in the virgin land of her spirit for the germination of the Word. She had conceived him in her heart, St Augustine tells us, before she conceived him in her body. As she felt the weight of the growth of Christ in her womb, she adapted her daily rhythms to those of her guest – she made a home for him. That is the secret of the enclosed garden – to make a home in the depths of our hearts, in our lives, for Christ.

> With great delight I sat in his shadow
> and his fruit was sweet to my taste. . . .
> Awake, O north wind,
> and come, O south wind!
> Blow upon my garden,
> let its spices flow. . . .
> I came to my garden, my sister, my bride,
> I gathered my myrrh with my spice,

I ate my honeycomb with my honey,
I drank my wine with my milk.
Eat, friends, drink,
and be drunk with love! (Sg 2:3, 4:16, 5:1)

The way in which we cultivate the inner life depends upon many things: above all our openness, our ability to listen, to receive, to be attentive, and to discern; our attitude to life in general and to God and the Church in particular; and our ability to trust all of these, not just one or another of them. For us, these attitudes are essential rudiments, indeed the necessary coordinates that enable a priestly vocation to flourish. It is never simply a personal desire.

Our world offers much that promises fulfilment and much of it good, but by its nature the fulfilment it brings can only be transitory. Life is too precious to be poured out on that which is not ultimately true. Like the Shulamite girl, Mary's heart remained faithful to the one whose desire for her, and through her for us, is so great that he comes among us – born in a city where there was much rejoicing and festivity, yet in circumstances that were poor and which needed the eyes of a lover to discern the greatness of that moment.

My beloved has gone down to his garden
to the beds of spices,
to graze in the gardens
and to gather lilies.

I am my beloved's and my beloved is mine;
he grazes among the lilies. (Sg 6:2–3)

As bishops and priests, we too have heard the Lord's call in the intimacy of our hearts – we have wrestled with it, experienced surprise and doubts, been challenged and ridiculed by others, but deep within us there is a joy, a great joy, as we ponder this mystery. Here we find our identity. The cell within us, the enclosed space that is only for the Lord, is where we hear his voice, where the graces are received and the virtues are born to burgeon into a passionate burning desire for Christ and for his Church. It is through this love affair that we will draw others to Christ. What we take to heart, what we nurture there, is the Word-made-flesh – a word that is not desiccated, nor stripped of love, but afire with a burning desire for the concerns of Christ. Pope Benedict XVI often said towards the end of his pontificate that the new evangelisation is not simply nor primarily a matter of battering home the moral truths, but of presenting the face of the living God by someone who knows the life-giving vitality of the incarnate Word and passionately loves the incarnate Word so much that he accepts the mission born in Baptism, to be sealed in priesthood, to make him known through love and loving service. That is our vocation. That is what we are called to, as so beautifully framed in the canticle:

Set me as a seal upon your heart,
as a seal upon your arm,
for love is strong as death,
jealousy is fierce as the grave.
Its flashes are flashes of fire,
the very flame of the Lord.
Many waters cannot quench love,
neither can floods drown it.
If a man offered for love
all the wealth of his house,
he would be utterly despised. (Sg 8:6–7)

St Bernard offers us wise counsel in one of his famous sermons on the Incarnation. Reflecting upon the Gospel of the Annunciation, he encourages us often to cultivate and call upon the name of Mary:

You, who see yourselves amid the tides of
    the world,
tossed by storms and tempests
rather than walking on the land,
do not turn your eyes away from this shining star,
unless you want to be overwhelmed by
    the hurricane.
If temptation storms,
or you fall upon the rocks of tribulation,
look to the star: Call upon Mary!
If you are tossed by the waves of pride
    or ambition,

detraction or envy,
look to the star, call upon Mary.
If anger or avarice or the desires of the flesh
dash against the ship of your soul,
turn your eyes to Mary.
If troubled by the enormity of your crimes,
ashamed of your guilty conscience,
terrified by dread of the judgment,
you begin to sink into the gulf of sadness
or the abyss of despair, think of Mary.
In dangers, in anguish, in doubt,
think of Mary, call upon Mary.
Let her name be ever on your lips, ever in
    your heart;
and the better to obtain the help of her prayers,
imitate the example of her life:
following her, you do not stray;
invoking her, you do not despair;
thinking of her, you do not wander;
upheld by her, you do not fall;
shielded by her, you do not fear;
guided by her, you do not grow weary;
favored by her, you reach the goal.
And thus do you experience in yourself
how good is that saying:
"And the Virgin's name was Mary."

Notes

tradition of praying towards the east: Basil the Great, *On the Holy Spirit* 27.66.

Eden as a symbol of the Church: Cyprian, *Letters* 73.11.

God's footsteps to help: Ephrem, *Commentary on Genesis* 2.24.

sound of God walking to induce a fear: John Chrysostom, *Homilies on Genesis* 17.3.4.

had they sought to repent: Ephrem, *Commentary on Genesis* 2.23.2.

a new tomb, which symbolises a womb: See, for example, Augustine, *Tractates on John* 120.5; Origen, *Contra Celsum* 2.69.

"Who was united with your Son in a death like his, may also be one with him in his Resurrection" (*qui complantatus fuit similitudini mortis Filii tui, simul fiat et resurrectionis ipsius*): Eucharistic Prayer III.

the new tree of life, the cross, bears the fruit which is Christ's Body: Tyconius, *Commentary on Apocalypse* 2.7.

CHAPTER II

"There is but an inch of difference between the cushioned chamber and the padded cell!": G.K. Chesterton, *Charles Dickens*, chap 6 (London: 1906).

"bringing to perfection his work in the world," so that "he might sanctify creation to the full" (*opus suum in mundo perficiens, omnem sanctificationem compleret*): Eucharistic Prayer IV.

"God has created me to do him some definite service . . .": John Henry Newman, "Meditations on Christian Doctrine: 7 March 1848," from *Meditations & Devotions*.

"Remember that God was already present in your dioceses . . .": Pope Francis, address to newly ordained bishops, 14 September 2017.

"the Apostle teaches us to pray everywhere, while the Saviour says 'Go into your room.' . . .": Ambrose, *On Cain and Abel* 1.9.38.

"And behold, you were within and I outside and it was there that I sought you [but you were not]" (*Et ecce intus eras et ego foris et ibi te quaerebam*): Augustine, *Confessions* 10.27.38.

CHAPTER III

God above and below, before and after: see "The Breastplate of St. Patrick" prayer.

the hypocrites' reward comes from those from whom they most desire to receive it: John Chrysostom, *Homilies on Matthew* 19.2.

"The Lord recalled to my mind the longing . . .": Julian of Norwich, *Revelations of Divine Love* (c. 1393).

"Faith demands adoration. . . .": Pope Francis, Homily on the Solemnity of the Epiphany, 6 January 2020.

"When Jesus teaches us the name 'Father' . . .": Jeremy Driscoll, *What Happens at Mass* (Chicago: Liturgy Training Publications, 2005), 112–113.

"What is meant if not that lost door . . .": Paul Claudel, *I Believe in God: A Meditation on the Apostles' Creed*, 244–245.

"Keep us alert, we pray, O Lord our God . . .": Roman Missal, Collect of Monday, First Week of Advent.

CHAPTER IV

"We have a high priest who is capable of sympathising with our weaknesses. . . . Jesus is like us. . . .": Pope Francis, Homily with survivors of Typhoon Haiyan (Yolanda), 17 January 2015.

"The great men and women of God were great intercessors. . . .": Pope Francis, *Evangelii Gaudium* 283.

Dies irae: The sequence is used as a hymn in the final week *per annum* of the Liturgy of the Hours.

"through the ministry of the Church": See the sacramental formula of absolution.

the sacrament of Penance is a true fountain of mercy and not a "torture chamber": Pope Francis, "General Audience," November 13, 2013.

"There is good reason for my solid hope in him . . .": Augustine, *Confessions* 10.43.69–70.

"Homo sum, humani nil a me alienum puto!" (I am a man, and I consider myself no alien to anything human!): Terence, *Heautontimorumenos* 77.

"It is not always wrong even to go, like Dante, to the brink . . .": G.K. Chesterton, *Alarms and Discursions* (1910).

CHAPTER V

"This, then, is to watch: to be detached from what is present, and to live in what is unseen": John Henry Newman, *Parochial and Plain Sermons* 4.22.

the Lord never sends anything to us that isn't good for our soul: See Jean Pierre de Caussade, *Abandonment to Divine Providence*.

'*exemplum*' and '*mysterium*' or '*sacramentum*': Leo the Great, *Sermons* 72.1. *Crucem Christi . . . et sacramentum est et exemplum*, Leo the Great, *Sermons* 72.2.

"the two richest and most intense months of my life, in which my highest values were so deeply confirmed. I have learned to love Westerbork": Etty Hillesum, *An Interrupted Life: The Diaries of Etty Hillesum 1941–1943* (New York: Washington Square Press, 1985).

"You put these words of mine into your ears!": Most translations of this saying are rather weak, e.g., 'take to heart' or 'listen to what I say'.

CHAPTER VI

"it was still dark" indicates to us the state of Mary's faith: Gregory the Great, *Forty Gospel Homilies* 22.

"The young women bearing incense hasten towards the dawn . . .": Romanus, Kontakion on the Resurrection 29:1–3.

'Cleopas, the brother of St Joseph': Eusebius, *Ecclesiastical History* 3.11.2; PG 20, 246–247.

"Every man goes through this period of crisis. . . .": Hermann Hesse, *Demian* (1919).

"Oh God, times are too hard for frail people like myself. . . .": Etty Hillesum, *An Interrupted Life: The Diaries of Etty Hillesum 1941–1943* (New York: Washington Square Press, 1985).

"They had given up hope. . . .": Augustine, *Sermons* 236A.4.

"her love revealed him to her, and her doubt prevented her from knowing him": Gregory the Great, *Forty Gospel Homilies* 25.

"Thus it happened that she alone saw him, she who had remained behind to seek him, simply because a true good act involves the virtue of perseverance": Gregory the Great, *Forty Gospel Homilies* 25.

"For the lips of Truth have said, 'the one who perseveres to the end will be saved'": Gregory the Great, *Forty Gospel Homilies* 25.

"the human heart has to be broken open before it can receive God . . .": Ruth Burrows, *Through Him, with Him, in Him: Meditations on the Liturgical Seasons* (London: Sheed & Ward, 1987), 124.

"You see then that you must not complain or run away in time of darkness . . .": Catherine of Siena, Letter T211/G88/ DT70.

Father Robert Thomas, a French Trappist monk of the last century, used an illustration . . . : Robert Thomas, *Passing from Self to God: A Cistercian Retreat* (Kalamazoo, MI: Cistercian Publications, 2006), 17.

"Made by God for himself": *Fecisti nos ad Te*, Augustine, *Confessions* 1.1.1.

CHAPTER VII

"From this point on my capacity to see was greater than words can show, which fail in the face of such seeing": Dante, *Paradiso* 33.55–57.

"in its depths I saw gathered, bound with love in one volume, what is scattered in gatherings through the universe!": Dante, *Paradiso* 33.85–87.

the whole of the universe is like a book written by God's finger: Hugh of St Victor, *De tribus diebus* 4; PL 176,814.

on the workers in the vineyard: John Chrysostom, *Homilies on Matthew* 64.3.

"The sheepfold of our holy Church receives goats together with lambs . . .": Gregory the Great, *Forty Gospel Homilies* 19.5.

"We are never more soul sick than when we become confused and find ourselves helpless to cope with a situation. That is the primary meaning of the prayer 'Send Your Radiant Light'": Alfred Delp, *Gesammelte Schriften*, Bd. 4 (ed. Hrsg. Von Roman Bleistein), Frankfurt, 1985. "Send your radiant light" is taken from the first stanza of *Veni Sancte Spiritus*.

story of St Francis and Brother Leo: See Éloi Leclerc, *The Wisdom of The Poor One of Assisi*.

"He is not touched by reality. And yet, in his mind, he can believe he possesses reality. For he has control over these images which he makes and he shapes them to his own will": Susan Griffin, *Pornography and Silence: Culture's Revenge Against Nature* (London, 1981), 122.

"It is the only thing we can do." "I see no alternative, each of us ought to destroy in himself all that he thinks he ought to destroy in others": Etty Hillesum, *An Interrupted Life: The*

Diaries of Etty Hillesum 1941–1943 (New York: Washington Square Press, 1985).

"Until you know deep inside that Jesus thirsts for you . . .": Mother Teresa, *Jesus Is My All in All: Praying with the "Saint of Calcutta"* (New York: Doubleday, 2008), 27; Joseph Langford, *Mother Teresa's Secret Fire* (Huntington, Indiana: Our Sunday Visitor, 2008), 56.

"the Minister of the Word must possess and pass on that knowledge of God which is not a mere deposit of doctrinal truths but a personal and living experience of the Mystery": Pope John Paul II, *Gift and Mystery*, 49.

the most effective and authentic teachers are those whose personal lives give testimony: Pope Paul VI, *Evangelii Nuntiandi* 41, 69, 76.

"I hear mankind say to the Creator . . .": Guerric of Igny, *Palm Sunday Sermon* 1:1.

CHAPTER VIII

dialogue on humility by Uriah Heep: Charles Dickens, *David Copperfield*, chap 39.

"in the Beatitudes something of the celestial grandeur breaks through. They are no mere formulas for superior ethics, but tidings of sacred and supreme reality's entry into the world": Romano Guardini, *The Lord*.

"The glory of God is man fully alive!" (*Gloria enim Dei est vivens homo*): Irenaeus of Lyon, *Against Heresies* 4.20.7. The quote continues, "*vita autem hominis visio Dei.*"

humility is not listed among the seven theological and cardinal virtues in the *Catechism*: See *CCC* 1804–1829 (*Faith, Hope, Charity, Prudence, Justice, Fortitude, Temperance*).

"grace perfects nature": Thomas Aquinas, *Summa theologiae* 1.1.8 ad 2.

"he became man so that we might become God": Athanasius, *On the Incarnation* 54.3. The Greek could be rendered, "He en-manned so that we might be deified".

"Self-knowledge is the dwelling in which we discover our own lowliness . . .": Catherine of Siena, Letter 141 to Don Giovanni de'Sabbatini da Bologna.

"consists in losing the memory of our personal 'salvation history' . . .": Pope Francis, address to the Roman Curia, 22 December 2014.

a humble man "will not be thinking about humility: he will not be thinking about himself at all": C.S. Lewis, *Mere Christianity*, Bk 3, chap 8, "The Great Sin".

on St Bernard: William of St-Thierry, *Vita prima Sancti Bernardi* 1.13.62.

the anointing that we receive as priests is not for ourselves: Pope Francis, Homily at the Chrism Mass on Holy Thursday, 17 April 2014.

"the traces of whatever arises there must be prudently considered. . . .": John Cassian, *Conferences* 1.22. Cassian is alluding to Ps 91:13b.

'more grievous are the consequences of anger than the causes of it': a popularized form taken from Marcus Aurelius, *Meditations* 11.16.8.

"For Christ belongs to those who are humble-minded": Pope Clement I, *First Letter to the Corinthians* 16.1–2.

the pride that changed angels into devils and of the humility that makes men equal to angels: Augustine, *Sermons* 198.

"We must be distinguished not by our clothing, but by what we really are": Cyril of Alexandria, *Commentary on Luke*, Sermon 33.

"A fool tries to look different: a clever man looks the same and is different": John Buchan, *The Thirty-Nine Steps*.

"Watch out for the double soul . . .": *The Shepherd of Hermas*, Mandate 9.9.

"That which we celebrated up to today is the birth of Christ, that which we celebrate today is our own birth": Guerric of Igny, *Sermon* 14.1.

"Listen at least, Naaman, to your servants . . .": Guerric of Igny, *Sermon* 14.6.7.

"My God, you have always taught humility by word and example . . .": Charles de Foucauld, Humility, Retreat at Nazareth, 1897, MH, 73–76. In ascribing a quote to St Augustine, he was intending to capture the spirit of Augustine's thought rather than his words; see his Letter to Dioscorus, *Letters* 118.3.22.

CHAPTER IX

"You are an enclosed garden, O Mother of God, an enclosed garden, a fountain sealed: arise, my love!" (*Hortus conclusus es, Dei Genetrix, hortus conclusus, fons signatus: surge, propera, amica mea!*): *Ordo Cantus Officii* (LEV, 2015), Assumption, 206.

"Truly I must love Him perfectly . . .": Bernard of Clairvaux, *Sermones in Cantica Canticorum* 20.

She had conceived him in her heart before she conceived him in her body (*Quae cum dixisset angelus, illa fide plena, et*

Christum prius mente quam ventre concipiens: Ecce, inquit, ancilla Domini . . .): Augustine, *Sermons* 215.4; PL 38, 1074.

"You, who see yourselves amid the tides of the world . . .": Bernard of Clairvaux, *Hom. II super Missus est* 2.17. Commonly known as *In Laudibus Virginis Matris.*

Word on Fire Catholic Ministries is a nonprofit global media apostolate that supports the work of Bishop Robert Barron and reaches millions of people to draw them into—or back to—the Catholic faith.

Word on Fire uses contemporary forms of media and innovative communication technologies to effectively share the Gospel via books, articles, videos, podcasts, and more.

Visit our website at *www.wordonfire.org* to learn more about our mission to proclaim Christ in the culture. Sign up to receive updates from Bishop Barron.